SKOPE TRAVEL GUIDE

2024 & 2025 Complete Companion To Explore The Greek Island In Western Aegean Sea Like A Local With Everything To Know, Travel Hacks, Itineraries & Map

Gianna McMillon

Copyright

© Gianna McMillon, 2024.

All rights reserved.

No part of this publication may be reproduced, distributed, or transmitted in any form or by any means, including photocopying, recording, or other electronic or mechanical methods, without the prior written permission of the publisher, except in the case of brief quotations embodied in critical reviews and certain other noncommercial uses permitted by copyright law.

All images, graphics, and content within this guide are either owned by Gianna McMillon or used with permission from their respective owners. Any trademarks, service marks, product names, or named features are assumed to be the property of their respective owners and are used only for reference. There is no implied endorsement if we use one of these terms. Unauthorized use of any content in this publication may violate copyright, trademark, and other laws.

About The Author

Gianna McMillon is an avid traveler and seasoned travel guide author who has spent over two decades exploring the far corners of the world. Born with an insatiable curiosity and a love for adventure, Gianna has transformed her passion for travel into a successful writing career, inspiring countless readers to embark on their own journeys.

Gianna's travel guides are renowned for their meticulous detail, vivid descriptions, and practical advice, making them essential companions for travelers of all kinds. Her expertise spans diverse destinations, from the bustling streets of Tokyo and the romantic boulevards of Paris to the serene landscapes of New Zealand and the exotic locales of Southeast Asia.

With a background in cultural anthropology and a flair for storytelling, Gianna brings a unique perspective to her writing. She delves beyond the typical tourist attractions, uncovering hidden gems and local secrets that offer readers an authentic and immersive experience. Her guides not only provide logistical insights but also enrich the travel experience with historical context, cultural nuances, and personal anecdotes.

Gianna's work has been featured in prominent travel magazines and online platforms, earning her a loyal following of readers who eagerly anticipate her next adventure. When she's not exploring new destinations, Gianna enjoys sharing her experiences through engaging talks and workshops, inspiring others to see the world with fresh eyes.

Whether you're a seasoned traveler or a first-time explorer, Gianna McMillon's travel guides will equip you with the knowledge and inspiration to make your journey unforgettable.

TABLE OF CONTENTS

Chapter 1 10
DISCOVER SKOPELOS 10
    The Hidden Gem Of The Aegean 10
    Quick Facts And History 15
    Why Skopelos Should Be Your 2024/2025 Travel List 19

Chapter 2 24
SPENDING WISELY: BUDGET TIPS FOR SKOPELOS 24
    What To Expect: Average Costs In Skopelos 24
    Best Places To Get Value For Money 32
    Saving On Accommodation And Dining ... 41
    Affordable Souvenirs And Local Crafts 46

Chapter 3 53
MOVING AROUND: EXPLORING SKOPELOS 53
    Getting To Skopelos: Ferries And Flights . 53
    Navigating The Island: Car Rentals And Public Transport 58
    Scenic Walks And Cycling Routes 63
    Boat Trips: Island Hopping And Coastal Cruises 69

Chapter 4 76
SLEEPING OVER: WHERE TO STAY 76
    Top Hotels For Every Budgets 76
    Charming Villas And Cozy Guesthouses .. 81

Unique Stays: Traditional Homes And Eco-lodges 86
Best Areas To Stay: Town, Beach Or Countryside? 91

Chapter 5 97
EATING: SAVORING THE FLAVORS OF SKOPELOS 97

Traditional Skopelos Dishes You Must Try97
Best Local Taverns, Cafes, and Fine Dining Spots 103
Fresh Seafood And Farm-to-Table Restaurants 109
Food Markets And Where To Find Local Ingredients 115

Chapter 6 121
ADVENTURES: SKOPELOS AT ITS WILDEST 121

Top Beaches: Sandy Spots And Secluded Coves 121
Hiking Trails With Stunning Views 129
Water Sports: Kayaking, Snorkeling And Sailing 137
Day Trips And Boat Excursions To Neighboring Islands 144

Chapter 7 153
STAYING SAFE AND GREEN 153

Health And Safety Tips For Travelers 153
Protecting The Environment: Eco-friendly Travel 158
Emergency Contacts And Medical Care in

5

Skopelos 167
Chapter 8 174
ESSENTIAL PLANNING: MAKE THE MOST OF YOUR TRIP 174
When To Visit: Best Times For Weather And Festivals 174
Travel Essentials: What To Pack For Skopelos 179
Getting Around: Tips For Renting Vehicles And Public Transit 184
Important Travel Documents And Insurance 188
Chapter 9 194
SAMPLED ITINERARIES FOR EVERY KIND OF TRAVELER 194
3-Day Itinerary: Quick Getaway Highlights 194
5-Day Itinerary: Relaxation And Adventure Combo 199
7-Day Itinerary: In-Depth Exploration Of Skopelos 205
Hidden Gems: Off-the-beaten-path Adventures 212
Chapter 10 219
ICONIC LANDMARKS AND MUST-SEE ATTRACTIONS 219
Agios Loannis Chapel: The Mamma Mia! Church 219
Skopelos Old Town: Cobblestone Streets And Historic Charm 223
The Venetian Castle: Panoramic Island Views 227

Monasteries Of Skopelos: Peaceful
Sanctuaries In The Hills...................231
Kastani Beach And Panormos: Cinematic
Beaches To Visit...........................235
Chapter 11 240
**WHAT NOT TO DO: AVOID THESE
COMMON PITFALLS 240**
Overcrowded Spots: Alternatives To Tourist
Traps 240
Cultural Missteps: What's Considered Rude
In Greece..................................244
Skipping Local: Why You Should Support
Skopelos Business....................247
CONCLUSION 252
Final Thoughts 252

```
         0     1     2     3
                      N. Miles
```

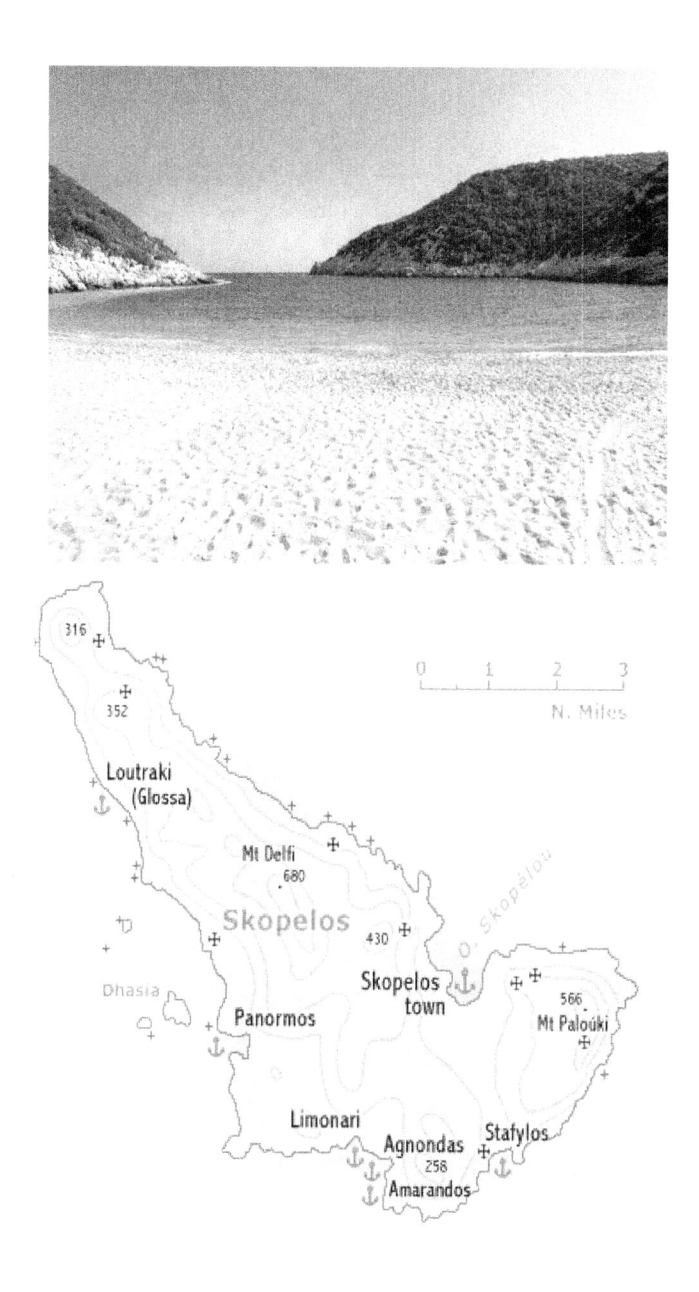

316

352

Loutraki
(Glossa)

Mt Delfi
680

Skopelos 430

Dhasia

Panormos

Skopelos town

566
Mt Paloúki

Limonari

Agnondas   Stafylos
   258
Amarandos

8

SKOPELOS MAP

Scan Me

We Promise It Will Be Easy

How To Scan Code

1. Open a QR code scanning app or feature on your device.

2. Position the QR code within the frame of your device's camera.

3. Wait for the app or feature to recognize and scan the QR code.

4. Once scanned, the app or feature will usually display the information or take appropriate action.

5. If necessary, interact with the scanned content as desired.

Chapter 1

DISCOVER SKOPELOS

The Hidden Gem Of The Aegean

Settled in the crystal-clear waters of the Aegean Sea, Skopelos is a hidden paradise that often escapes the radar of mainstream tourism, making it one of Greece's most captivating and serene destinations. Part of the Northern Sporades archipelago, Skopelos is known for its unspoiled beauty, lush landscapes, and a rich cultural heritage that blends seamlessly with its stunning natural scenery.

While nearby islands like Skiathos and Alonissos have their own charm, Skopelos offers something truly unique: an authentic Greek experience where travelers can immerse themselves in the quiet charm of island life, explore pristine beaches, and wander through cobblestone streets lined with traditional whitewashed houses adorned with colorful bougainvillea.

A Pristine Island Oasis

Skopelos is often dubbed the "greenest island in Greece" due to its dense forests, which cover nearly 80% of the island. Towering pine trees stretch down to the coastline, meeting azure waters in a breathtaking contrast. This makes Skopelos an ideal destination for nature lovers, offering a perfect blend of beach and forest. The island boasts over 360 churches and monasteries, many of which are perched on hillsides or nestled deep in the countryside, offering visitors a peaceful retreat and a sense of timelessness.

Skopelos has managed to preserve its traditional character and remains largely unspoiled by mass tourism. Visitors are greeted with friendly locals, authentic Greek cuisine, and a slower pace of life that encourages relaxation and exploration.

Skopelos Town: A Blend of History and Charm

Skopelos Town, the island's capital, is a beautiful labyrinth of narrow alleys, old Venetian-style buildings, and quaint little squares. The town stretches from the port up the hillside, offering breathtaking views of the harbor below. The architecture is a mix of traditional island homes with red-tiled roofs and Venetian influences, dating back to the island's storied past under Venetian rule.

Wandering through Skopelos Town feels like stepping back in time, with each corner revealing hidden gems such as ancient churches, local artisan shops, and cozy tavernas serving fresh seafood and local specialties. The waterfront is dotted with cafes and restaurants, making it a perfect spot to enjoy a leisurely meal while watching the boats drift by.

Mamma Mia! and Skopelos' Global Fame
For many, Skopelos is synonymous with the film Mamma Mia!, which was largely shot on the island in 2008. The film's success catapulted Skopelos to international fame, drawing visitors eager to see the iconic locations, such as the stunning Agios Ioannis Chapel, perched high on a rock overlooking the sea. The cinematic allure of Skopelos is undeniable, with its dramatic landscapes and picturesque beaches offering a perfect backdrop for adventure and romance.

However, despite the influx of tourists drawn by the movie's popularity, Skopelos has managed to maintain its tranquil, unspoiled character. Rather than becoming overrun, the island has balanced its newfound fame with a commitment to preserving its natural beauty and traditional way of life.

Skopelos' Unique Culture and Traditions

Beyond its natural beauty, Skopelos is steeped in a rich cultural heritage. The island has a long tradition of shipbuilding, and remnants of its maritime past can still be found in the island's museums and old shipyards. Folk music and dance are also integral to the island's cultural fabric, with festivals and celebrations often featuring traditional Skopelos songs and dances, especially during the summer months.

Handcrafted pottery, ceramics, and woodwork are part of Skopelos' artisanal tradition, and visitors can often find unique, handmade souvenirs in the local shops. The island's religious festivals, such as the Feast of the Assumption, are celebrated with great enthusiasm, offering travelers a chance to witness the island's deep-rooted faith and community spirit.

Untouched Beaches and Natural Wonders

One of Skopelos' greatest attractions is its pristine beaches. Whether you're looking for lively beach bars or secluded, peaceful coves, Skopelos has something for every kind of traveler. Beaches like Kastani, Panormos, and Milia are renowned for their clear waters and stunning surroundings, perfect for swimming, snorkeling, and sunbathing. For those seeking a more secluded experience, hidden gems like Perivoliou and Hovolo offer tranquility and unspoiled beauty.

In addition to its beaches, Skopelos is a paradise for hikers. The island is crisscrossed with ancient footpaths that take you through forests, olive groves, and vineyards, leading to breathtaking views from mountaintops or quiet moments in centuries-old monasteries.

Why Skopelos Should Be Your Next Destination
While many Greek islands have become crowded and commercialized, Skopelos remains a sanctuary for those seeking an authentic, peaceful escape. Its blend of natural beauty, rich cultural heritage, and warm hospitality makes it the perfect destination for travelers looking to experience Greece at its most genuine. Whether you're exploring its ancient churches, relaxing on a quiet beach, or savoring local delicacies at a family-run taverna, Skopelos offers a truly magical experience that will leave you enchanted long after you've left its shores.

Skopelos is not just an island, but a journey into a simpler, more beautiful way of life, making it a must-visit for anyone seeking a unique and unforgettable Aegean adventure.

Quick Facts And History

Quick Facts
- Location: Northern Sporades, Aegean Sea, Greece
- Size: 96 square kilometers (37 square miles)
- Population: Approximately 5,000 permanent residents
- Main Town: Skopelos Town (Chora)
- Official Language: Greek
- Currency: Euro (€)
- Time Zone: Eastern European Time (EET) - UTC+2, and UTC+3 in summer (EEST)
- Famous For: Lush landscapes, traditional architecture, Mamma Mia! filming locations, unspoiled beaches, monasteries

A Glimpse Into Skopelos' History
Skopelos has a rich and diverse history that stretches back thousands of years, with evidence of settlement as far back as the Bronze Age. According to ancient Greek mythology, the island was founded by Staphylos, son of the god Dionysus (the god of wine) and Ariadne, which ties Skopelos

to wine production and a longstanding tradition of viticulture.

Prehistoric and Ancient Period
Archaeological findings indicate that Skopelos has been inhabited since the Neolithic era, with early settlers establishing agricultural and maritime traditions that would shape the island's future. By the 8th century BCE, Skopelos (known as Peparethos in antiquity) had become an important city-state. Peparethos was renowned for its wine, which was exported throughout the ancient Greek world. Coins minted on the island bear the symbol of the vine, reinforcing the importance of winemaking to Skopelos' early economy.

Roman and Byzantine Periods
During the Roman era, Skopelos fell under Roman control, though it remained a relatively peaceful and prosperous island due to its strategic location in the Aegean Sea. The island also flourished during the Byzantine era, as seen by the construction of many churches and monasteries, some of which still stand today. These religious sites became centers of local culture and spirituality, and many have continued to serve as pilgrimage sites.

Venetian Rule and Pirate Raids

In the 13th century, Skopelos was conquered by the Venetians, who ruled the island for several centuries. This period left a distinct Venetian mark on the island's architecture, particularly in Skopelos Town, where many of the old buildings have a blend of Venetian and Greek influences.

However, this period also brought challenges, as Skopelos became a target for pirate attacks due to its position along trade routes. The island's inhabitants built fortified homes and churches to protect themselves from these raids, some of which can still be seen today.

Ottoman Era and Liberation
Like much of Greece, Skopelos came under Ottoman control in the 15th century. However, the island managed to maintain a degree of autonomy, largely due to its remote location and small size. Skopelos continued to thrive agriculturally, with olive oil production becoming a major part of the island's economy.

The island played an active role in the Greek War of Independence (1821-1829), after which Skopelos, along with the rest of Greece, gained independence from the Ottoman Empire. Following liberation, the island entered a new phase of growth and development.

Modern Era and the Rise of Tourism
Throughout the 20th century, Skopelos remained a quiet, agricultural island, relatively untouched by the mass tourism that was transforming other parts of Greece. It wasn't until the late 20th century that tourism began to take off, although Skopelos has maintained its traditional character and avoided the overdevelopment seen on more popular islands.

In 2008, Skopelos gained international fame when it served as a primary filming location for the Hollywood musical Mamma Mia!. The movie showcased the island's natural beauty, including its stunning beaches and iconic Agios Ioannis Chapel, to a global audience. This brought a surge of visitors, though the island has managed to balance tourism with preservation of its natural and cultural heritage.

Today, Skopelos is celebrated for its lush greenery, tranquil lifestyle, and traditional Greek charm, making it a must-visit destination for travelers seeking an authentic Aegean experience. Its history is still visible in its architecture, monasteries, and local traditions, offering a unique glimpse into the island's storied past.

18

Why Skopelos Should Be Your 2024/2025 Travel List

Skopelos offers a unique and authentic Greek island experience that stands out in an increasingly crowded travel landscape. While many islands in the Aegean have embraced mass tourism, Skopelos has managed to retain its traditional charm and natural beauty, making it a perfect destination for those seeking a serene yet captivating adventure. Here's why Skopelos should be at the top of your 2024/2025 travel list:

1. Unspoiled Natural Beauty: Greece's Greenest Island

Skopelos is often referred to as Greece's greenest island, and for good reason. Nearly 80% of the island is covered in pine forests, olive groves, and fruit orchards, creating a lush landscape that is a refreshing contrast to the rocky, arid terrain found on many other Greek islands. The pine trees stretch down to the coastline, where they meet the island's clear, turquoise waters, forming an unforgettable natural panorama. Skopelos' dense greenery, combined with its pristine beaches and rugged cliffs, offers visitors a rare opportunity to experience nature at its most vibrant.

2. Idyllic Beaches and Crystal-Clear Waters

Skopelos boasts some of the most beautiful beaches in Greece, from organized, family-friendly spots to hidden, secluded coves. Beaches like Panormos, Kastani, and Milia are renowned for their soft sands and shimmering waters, ideal for swimming, snorkeling, or simply lounging in the sun. For those seeking more off-the-beaten-path locations, quiet coves like Perivoliou and Hovolo offer peace and solitude, surrounded by dramatic cliffs and tranquil seas. The variety of beaches ensures that every traveler can find their perfect spot to relax and unwind.

3. Authentic Greek Island Experience

Unlike its more tourist-heavy neighbors, Skopelos has preserved its traditional character, making it a perfect destination for those looking for an authentic Greek island experience. Skopelos Town, with its charming whitewashed houses, terracotta roofs, and winding cobblestone streets, is a place where time seems to have stood still. The island is dotted with family-run tavernas, cozy cafes, and artisan shops, offering a genuine taste of local life and culture. Visitors can stroll through the old town, visit centuries-old monasteries, and enjoy warm hospitality that feels intimate and personal.

4. Rich History and Cultural Heritage

Skopelos' history stretches back thousands of years, from its days as the ancient city-state of Peparethos to its Venetian and Byzantine periods. The island's rich cultural heritage is evident in its architecture, with over 360 churches and monasteries spread across the landscape. Many of these historic sites offer incredible views and peaceful retreats, perfect for those interested in exploring Skopelos' spiritual and historical roots. The island's strong ties to Greek folklore, music, and dance are also celebrated through festivals and cultural events throughout the year, giving visitors a chance to immerse themselves in local traditions.

5. A Haven for Outdoor Adventures
Skopelos is an outdoor lover's paradise. The island's hiking trails lead through lush forests, past ancient monasteries, and up to hilltops with sweeping views of the Aegean Sea. Whether you're an experienced hiker or just looking for a scenic walk, there are trails for every level of fitness. Skopelos' coastal waters also offer plenty of opportunities for kayaking, paddleboarding, and snorkeling, while boat tours allow travelers to explore nearby islands and hidden bays. For those looking to balance relaxation with adventure, Skopelos is the perfect destination.

6. The Magic of "Mamma Mia!"

Fans of the film Mamma Mia! will instantly recognize many of Skopelos' stunning locations. The iconic Agios Ioannis Chapel, perched on a rock high above the sea, and the breathtaking beaches of Kastani and Glysteri featured prominently in the movie, making Skopelos a must-visit for film enthusiasts. While the movie has drawn many visitors to the island, Skopelos has maintained its authentic appeal and avoided becoming overly commercialized, ensuring that its cinematic magic remains intact for visitors.

7. Sustainable and Eco-Friendly Travel

For travelers looking to reduce their environmental footprint, Skopelos is an excellent choice. The island has long embraced sustainable practices, from eco-friendly accommodations to initiatives aimed at preserving its natural environment. Visitors can enjoy green activities like hiking, cycling, and sailing, while supporting local businesses that prioritize sustainability. Skopelos' commitment to protecting its natural beauty makes it a great destination for environmentally-conscious travelers who want to experience the island's wonders without contributing to over-tourism.

8. Year-Round Appeal

While Skopelos is a popular summer destination, the island's charm extends beyond the peak season.

Spring and autumn offer milder temperatures, making it an ideal time for outdoor activities like hiking and sightseeing without the crowds. The island's forests burst into life in the spring, while the warm autumn months are perfect for exploring Skopelos' rich history and culture at a leisurely pace. Even in winter, the island offers a quiet, peaceful atmosphere, perfect for those seeking an off-season retreat in an idyllic setting.

Whether you're a nature enthusiast, history buff, film fan, or simply looking for an escape from the usual tourist hotspots, Skopelos has something special to offer. Its unspoiled beauty, authentic charm, and diverse experiences make it a must-see destination for 2024 and 2025. With its balance of tranquility and adventure, Skopelos promises a truly unforgettable Greek island experience that you'll cherish for years to come.

Chapter 2

SPENDING WISELY: BUDGET TIPS FOR SKOPELOS

What To Expect: Average Costs In Skopelos

Skopelos is a perfect destination for travelers who want to enjoy an authentic Greek island experience without the exorbitant price tags of more commercialized islands like Mykonos or Santorini. However, understanding the average costs on the island can help you budget wisely and make the most of your trip, whether you're traveling on a tight budget or planning to splurge. Here's a breakdown of what you can expect to spend in Skopelos, from accommodation to meals and transportation.

1. Accommodation Costs

Skopelos offers a wide range of accommodations, from budget-friendly options like guesthouses and self-catering apartments to more luxurious stays in boutique hotels and villas. Your choice of accommodation will significantly affect your overall spending, but there's something for every budget.

- Budget (Hostels and Guesthouses): €30 - €60 per night
  For travelers on a budget, simple guesthouses, small family-run hotels, or self-catering apartments are great options. These often come with basic amenities but offer comfort and cleanliness in a more modest setting.

- Mid-Range (Hotels and Apartments): €70 - €120 per night
  For those seeking a bit more comfort without going overboard, mid-range hotels and apartments provide a balance of quality and value. Expect spacious rooms, beautiful views, and amenities like Wi-Fi, air conditioning, and breakfast.

- Luxury (Boutique Hotels and Villas): €150 - €400+ per night

If you're looking for an upscale experience, Skopelos has some exquisite boutique hotels and private villas, particularly along the coastline. Luxury accommodations often feature private pools, sea views, and high-end services that ensure a memorable stay.

2. Food and Drink Costs
Skopelos is known for its delicious local cuisine, and you can enjoy fresh, high-quality food at reasonable prices. Whether dining in a local taverna or grabbing a quick bite at a bakery, you'll find a variety of options that cater to different tastes and budgets.

- Casual Dining (Tavernas and Cafes): €10 - €20 per person
   Traditional tavernas are the heart of Skopelos' dining scene, offering hearty portions of fresh seafood, grilled meats, and local specialties like the famous Skopelos cheese pie (tiropita). A meal at a typical taverna, including a starter, main course, and a glass of wine or beer, usually costs around €15 per person.

- Mid-Range Restaurants: €20 - €40 per person
   For a more refined dining experience, mid-range restaurants offer delicious dishes with a touch of elegance, often featuring fresh, locally-sourced

ingredients. Expect to pay around €25 to €35 for a full meal with drinks.

- High-End Dining: €50+ per person

Skopelos also boasts a few upscale dining options, perfect for a special night out. These restaurants typically offer gourmet versions of traditional Greek dishes or innovative fusion cuisine, and a meal can cost €50 or more per person, especially if you indulge in a full multi-course experience or fine wine.

- Street Food and Snacks: €3 - €8

For quick, inexpensive meals, bakeries and street vendors offer options like gyros, souvlaki, and pastries. A simple snack or takeaway meal will set you back around €3 to €8, perfect for a cheap and tasty lunch on the go.

3. Transportation Costs

Getting around Skopelos is relatively affordable, especially compared to more tourist-heavy islands. Whether you're using public transportation, renting a vehicle, or hopping on a boat, there are several options to suit your travel style.

- Public Buses: €2 - €3 per ride

Public buses are the most economical way to get around Skopelos, with routes connecting major towns, beaches, and attractions. Tickets generally cost between €2 and €3 per ride, depending on the distance. During the summer season, buses run more frequently to accommodate tourists.

- Taxis: €8 - €30 per ride
Taxis are convenient for short trips around the island. A short trip within Skopelos Town might cost around €8, while longer rides to more distant beaches or attractions could range from €20 to €30. Taxi fares increase at night or during holidays.

- Car or Scooter Rentals:
  - Scooter Rental: €20 - €35 per day
Renting a scooter is a budget-friendly option for solo travelers or couples, and it's a great way to explore the island's winding roads and remote beaches. Prices typically start around €20 to €35 per day.

  - Car Rental: €40 - €70 per day
Renting a car gives you the freedom to explore the island at your own pace. Depending on the season and vehicle type, daily rates range from €40 to €70. Keep in mind that petrol costs are additional (around €2 per liter).

- Boat Tours and Ferries:
  - Boat Tours: €25 - €60 per person

Day trips and boat tours to nearby islands or secluded beaches are popular activities in Skopelos. Prices for organized tours range from €25 to €60 per person, depending on the duration and services provided (some include meals or drinks).

- Ferry to Skopelos: €15 - €30 per person (one way)

Ferries from Volos, Skiathos, or Alonissos to Skopelos are the primary way to reach the island. Ticket prices vary based on the port of departure and the type of ferry (standard or high-speed).

4. Activities and Attractions

While many of Skopelos' natural attractions, like hiking trails and beaches, are free to explore, there are some activities and excursions that come with a price. However, most are relatively affordable.

- Beach Rentals (Sunbeds and Umbrellas): €5 - €10 per day

Some of the more popular beaches charge for sunbeds and umbrellas. On organized beaches like Panormos and Kastani, expect to pay around €5 to €10 for a set.

- Hiking and Nature Walks: Free

Skopelos offers a network of hiking trails that are free to access, providing stunning views of the island's landscapes, forests, and coastlines. Popular routes lead to hilltop monasteries, hidden coves, and panoramic viewpoints.

- Guided Tours (Cultural or Nature): €30 - €50 per person

For a more immersive experience, guided tours are available to explore the island's history, wildlife, or specific film locations from Mamma Mia!. These tours typically cost between €30 and €50 per person.

- Museums and Historical Sites: €2 - €5 entry fee

Skopelos has a few small museums, such as the Folklore Museum of Skopelos, with nominal entry fees around €2 to €5.

5. Shopping and Souvenirs

Shopping in Skopelos is largely focused on local craftsmanship and artisanal goods. Whether you're looking for handcrafted pottery, olive oil, or traditional Greek jewelry, prices are fairly reasonable.

- Handcrafted Pottery or Artisanal Souvenirs: €5 - €30

Locally made pottery, textiles, and small crafts are popular souvenirs. Prices range from €5 for smaller items like keychains or mugs, to €30 for more intricate pieces.

- Olive Oil, Honey, and Local Products: €5 - €15

Skopelos is known for its high-quality olive oil, honey, and other local food products. A bottle of olive oil or a jar of honey typically costs between €5 and €15, making them affordable and meaningful gifts or mementos.

Budgeting Tips for Skopelos

1. Visit in the Shoulder Season: Prices for accommodation, food, and activities tend to drop significantly in May, June, September, and October, making it an ideal time for budget-conscious travelers.

2. Opt for Self-Catering: Skopelos has excellent local markets where you can buy fresh produce, bread, and cheese. Staying in self-catering accommodations and preparing some of your meals can help you save money.

3. Use Public Transport: Instead of renting a car or relying on taxis, the affordable public bus system is a great way to reach the island's major attractions and beaches.

4. Explore Free Activities: Many of Skopelos' best experiences, like hiking, swimming, and exploring

its charming towns, are free or very low-cost. Take advantage of these to keep your budget in check.

By planning carefully and knowing what to expect, you can enjoy Skopelos without overspending, making it a fantastic destination for every kind of traveler.

Best Places To Get Value For Money

While Skopelos offers a luxurious escape with its scenic beauty and traditional charm, it's also an island where travelers can find excellent value for money without sacrificing quality. Whether you're looking for accommodations, dining options, or activities, Skopelos has plenty of affordable alternatives that allow you to enjoy your stay while sticking to a budget.

1. Budget-Friendly Accommodation

Skopelos has a variety of accommodation options that offer comfort, beautiful views, and great locations without breaking the bank. Here are some of the best budget and mid-range accommodations that provide excellent value.

- Evlalia Studios & Villas

Located just a short walk from Skopelos Town, this family-run complex offers self-catering studios and villas surrounded by olive trees and stunning sea views. The accommodations are spacious and equipped with kitchenettes, allowing guests to save money by preparing their own meals. Prices are reasonable, especially in the shoulder season, making it a great value for families or groups.

- Aegeon Hotel

This small, budget-friendly hotel in Skopelos Town is perfect for those who want a central location without a high price tag. With comfortable rooms, a peaceful garden, and free Wi-Fi, the Aegeon Hotel is ideal for solo travelers or couples looking for a clean and convenient place to stay. Rooms start at affordable rates, especially in off-peak months.

- Dolphin Hotel

Situated in the heart of Skopelos Town, Dolphin Hotel provides simple yet comfortable accommodations at a great price. It offers easy access to local attractions, restaurants, and shops, making it an excellent base for exploring the island. The hotel features a pool and a communal breakfast area, all for an affordable nightly rate.

- Amalia Hotel

This family-run hotel is located in a quiet part of Skopelos Town, offering rooms with private balconies overlooking the harbor. The hotel has a traditional Greek feel with clean and comfortable rooms, and it's known for its friendly service. Its central location means you're never far from the town's main attractions, and the prices are very reasonable.

2. Affordable Dining: Where to Eat Well for Less

Skopelos has a wide range of dining options, from casual tavernas to higher-end restaurants. If you're looking to eat well without overspending, there are plenty of places where you can enjoy delicious local food at a great price.

- Taverna Peparithos

Located near the harbor in Skopelos Town, Taverna Peparithos is a fantastic choice for those looking to experience traditional Greek cuisine at an affordable price. The taverna serves hearty portions of grilled meats, seafood, and classic Greek dishes like moussaka and souvlaki. The casual, laid-back atmosphere makes it a popular choice for both locals and tourists.

- Anna's Restaurant

Situated in the charming alleys of Skopelos Town, Anna's Restaurant is a hidden gem offering authentic Greek home-cooking at great prices. Known for its generous portions and traditional dishes like lamb with lemon and baked aubergine, it's a favorite for budget-conscious travelers who want to enjoy local flavors without overspending.

- To Rodi (The Pomegranate)

This small, family-run restaurant in Glossa offers fantastic value for money with its homemade dishes and warm hospitality. Serving a variety of Greek specialties like tzatziki, grilled sardines, and Skopelos cheese pie, To Rodi offers affordable meals with a view of the beautiful sunset over the Aegean. It's perfect for those visiting the northern part of the island.

- Agnanti

Located in the village of Glossa, Agnanti offers spectacular views of the sea and neighboring islands, as well as excellent food at reasonable prices. It's slightly more upscale but still offers good value, with a mix of traditional Greek and creative dishes. Agnanti is a great spot for a romantic dinner without the high price tag of a luxury restaurant.

- Kymata Tavern

Situated on the waterfront in Skopelos Town, Kymata Tavern is known for its fresh seafood and local specialties. The prices are very reasonable for a restaurant in such a prime location, and you can enjoy dishes like grilled octopus, fried calamari, and Skopelos-style fish stew while watching the boats in the harbor.

- Glyfoneri Taverna

Located near Glyfoneri Beach, this taverna is a favorite among locals for its simple, fresh, and affordable meals. Offering a range of grilled meats, fresh fish, and Greek salads, it's a great option for those spending the day at the beach. The taverna is family-run and known for its friendly service and rustic atmosphere.

3. Transportation: Moving Around on a Budget

Getting around Skopelos doesn't have to be expensive. The island has a variety of affordable transportation options that allow you to explore without the need for a rental car.

- Public Bus Service

Skopelos has a reliable public bus system that connects major towns and beaches, making it easy to get around the island on a budget. Bus fares are typically €2 - €3 per ride, depending on the distance. The buses run frequently during the summer, and the routes cover popular destinations like Panormos, Milia Beach, and Glossa.

- Scooter and Bicycle Rentals

For travelers who want more flexibility, renting a scooter or bicycle is an economical way to explore the island. Scooter rentals start at around €20 per day, and they are a great option for visiting remote beaches or driving through the island's scenic routes. Bicycles can be rented for around €10 to €15 per day, making it a budget-friendly and eco-friendly way to get around.

- Walking and Hiking

One of the best ways to explore Skopelos without spending any money is by walking or hiking. The island has several beautiful hiking trails that take you through pine forests, up to hilltop monasteries, and along the coastline. Walking allows you to take in the island's natural beauty at your own pace and is a great option for budget-conscious travelers who love the outdoors.

4. Free and Low-Cost Attractions
While Skopelos has a few paid attractions, many of the island's most beautiful and memorable experiences are free or very affordable. Here are some of the best value-for-money activities on the island:

- Beaches
Skopelos is famous for its stunning beaches, many of which are free to access. Whether you're visiting the organized beaches like Panormos and Kastani, or exploring more secluded spots like Hovolo and Perivoliou, you'll find plenty of options to spend a day by the sea without spending a cent. Some organized beaches charge for sunbeds and umbrellas, but prices are generally around €5 to €10.

- Hiking to Monasteries
Skopelos is home to several beautiful monasteries, many of which are located on scenic hillsides or mountaintops. These sites are free to visit and offer a peaceful retreat with incredible views. Popular monasteries include Monastery of Agios Riginos

and Monastery of Evangelistria, both of which can be reached via hiking trails that provide great opportunities to explore the island's lush landscape.

- Agios Ioannis Chapel (Mamma Mia! Church)

The famous Agios Ioannis Chapel, perched on a rock high above the sea, is a must-see for Mamma Mia! fans and nature lovers alike. The chapel itself is free to visit, and the climb up the rock is rewarded with breathtaking views of the Aegean Sea. This iconic spot is a great example of a spectacular experience that doesn't cost a thing.

- Skopelos Folklore Museum

For a small entry fee of around €3, visitors can explore the Skopelos Folklore Museum in Skopelos Town, which showcases the island's rich cultural heritage, traditional costumes, and local crafts. It's an affordable and educational way to learn about the island's history and way of life.

- Cultural Festivals and Events

Throughout the year, Skopelos hosts various festivals and cultural events that are free or low-cost to attend. The Skopelos Dance Festival and local religious festivals are great opportunities to experience traditional Greek music, dance, and food, all while mingling with locals and other visitors.

5. Shopping: Affordable Souvenirs
Shopping in Skopelos doesn't have to be expensive. Many of the island's shops sell unique, locally-made products that offer excellent value for money. Here's where you can find affordable yet meaningful souvenirs:

- Local Artisanal Shops
  Skopelos is known for its pottery, handmade textiles, and other artisanal crafts. Many local artists sell their work at reasonable prices in the shops of Skopelos Town and Glossa. You can find beautiful handcrafted pottery starting at around €10, making it an affordable and special souvenir to take home.

- Olive Oil and Honey
  Skopelos produces some of the finest olive oil and honey in Greece, and you can purchase these local products directly from farms or markets. A bottle of high-quality olive oil or a jar of honey costs around €5 to €15, making them an affordable and authentic gift or keepsake.

- Greek Sandals and Jewelry
  Local shops in Skopelos Town offer traditional Greek sandals, jewelry, and accessories at fair prices. Sandals typically cost between €20 and €40,

while handmade jewelry can be found for as little as €15, offering great value for a high-quality item.

By choosing budget-friendly accommodations, dining at local tavernas, utilizing public transportation, and exploring the island's free and low-cost attractions, travelers can experience all the magic of Skopelos without overspending. Skopelos is a hidden gem where value and quality go hand in hand, allowing you to make the most of your trip without compromising on experience.

Saving On Accommodation And Dining

Skopelos offers a range of options for travelers looking to save money on accommodation and dining while still enjoying a memorable Greek island experience. With some strategic planning and insider tips, you can enjoy the island's beauty and charm without stretching your budget. Here's how you can save on accommodation and dining in Skopelos:

Saving on Accommodation
1. Book in Advance
- Early Reservations: Booking your accommodation several months in advance often leads to lower rates and better availability. This is especially important during peak tourist season

(July and August), when prices can surge and options become limited.

- Special Deals and Discounts: Many hotels and guesthouses offer early bird discounts or promotional rates. Keep an eye out for these deals on booking websites and directly on hotel websites.

2. Consider Off-Peak Travel
   - Travel in Shoulder Seasons: Visiting Skopelos in the shoulder seasons (late spring or early autumn) can save you money. Prices for accommodations typically drop, and you'll avoid the summer crowds. The weather remains pleasant, and many attractions are less crowded.
   - Winter Visits: If you're open to a quieter experience, visiting in winter can also be cost-effective. While some businesses may be closed, you can find significant discounts on accommodation.

3. Opt for Self-Catering Accommodations
   - Apartments and Studios: Self-catering options such as studios and apartments often offer better value for money compared to hotels. With kitchen facilities, you can prepare your own meals, saving on dining expenses. Many self-catering options also include essential amenities like Wi-Fi and air conditioning.

- Grocery Shopping: Utilize local markets and grocery stores to buy fresh produce, bread, and other staples. Cooking your own meals or preparing simple breakfasts can significantly reduce your overall food costs.

4. Explore Guesthouses and Family-Run Hotels
  - Guesthouses: Family-run guesthouses and small hotels often offer lower rates and a more personalized experience. These accommodations are usually clean, comfortable, and provide a warm local touch. Prices are generally lower compared to larger, more commercial hotels.
  - Local Recommendations: Ask locals for recommendations on budget-friendly guesthouses. They often have insider knowledge of hidden gems that may not be widely advertised.

5. Check for Special Offers and Packages
  - Package Deals: Look for package deals that include accommodation and some additional perks, such as meals or local tours. These packages can offer good value and make budgeting easier.
  - Discounts for Extended Stays: Some accommodations offer discounts for longer stays. If you plan to stay for a week or more, inquire about special rates for extended visits.

Saving on Dining

1. Dine at Local Taverns and Cafes
   - Traditional Taverns: Local taverns and cafes often offer delicious Greek food at reasonable prices. Look for places frequented by locals, as they tend to offer better value compared to tourist spots.
   - Daily Specials: Many tavernas have daily specials or set menus that provide good value. These specials often feature local dishes and are priced lower than a la carte options.

2. Try Street Food and Bakeries
   - Gyros and Souvlaki: Street food such as gyros and souvlaki is not only tasty but also very affordable. Many small vendors and casual eateries offer these quick meals for a fraction of the price of a full restaurant meal.
   - Bakery Treats: Greek bakeries offer a variety of pastries and snacks at low prices. Items like spanakopita (spinach pie) and tiropita (cheese pie) are delicious and budget-friendly options for breakfast or a light lunch.

3. Take Advantage of Lunch Deals
   - Lunch Menus: Many restaurants offer lunch specials or set menus that are more economical than dinner options. Enjoying a substantial meal during lunchtime can help you save on dining expenses.
   - Early Bird Specials: Some restaurants provide discounts for early diners. If you're flexible with

meal times, taking advantage of these early bird specials can result in significant savings.

4. Avoid Tourist Traps
   - Menu Prices: Be cautious of restaurants with prominently displayed menus and flashy signs targeting tourists. These places often charge higher prices. Instead, seek out restaurants that blend in with the local environment and are popular with residents.
   - Avoiding High-Traffic Areas: Dining establishments located in high-traffic tourist areas or directly on the waterfront often have inflated prices. Opt for eateries located slightly off the beaten path for better value.

5. Enjoy Picnics and Beachside Meals
   - Pack Your Own Meals: Prepare picnics with items purchased from local markets or grocery stores. Enjoy your meal at one of Skopelos' beautiful beaches or scenic spots. It's a cost-effective way to have a meal with a view and avoid the higher costs of dining out.
   - Portable Grills: If your accommodation allows, consider using a portable grill or barbecue to cook meals. Many self-catering accommodations have outdoor spaces where you can grill and enjoy a meal al fresco.

6. Participate in Local Food Festivals
   - Festivals and Markets: Keep an eye out for local food festivals and markets, which often feature affordable and delicious food from various vendors. These events offer a chance to sample a variety of local dishes at reasonable prices.

7. Utilize Online Reviews and Recommendations
   - Review Sites: Check online review sites and forums for recommendations on budget-friendly dining options. Reviews from other travelers can help you find hidden gems and avoid overpriced establishments.
   - Social Media: Follow local social media pages or food bloggers who provide insights into the best value-for-money dining experiences on the island.

By following these tips, you can make the most of your budget while experiencing the rich flavors and hospitality of Skopelos. Whether you're savoring a meal at a local taverna or preparing your own dishes in a self-catering accommodation, Skopelos offers many ways to enjoy a fulfilling and affordable stay.

Affordable Souvenirs And Local Crafts

Bringing home souvenirs and local crafts from Skopelos doesn't have to mean splurging. The island offers a range of affordable and authentic mementos that capture the essence of Greek culture and craftsmanship.

1. Handmade Pottery
- Local Pottery Shops: Skopelos is known for its beautiful handmade pottery, which is often created by local artisans using traditional techniques. You can find charming ceramic pieces such as mugs, bowls, and plates in various shops throughout Skopelos Town and the village of Glossa.
- Affordability: Prices for small pottery items like mugs and small bowls start at around €10 to €20. Larger pieces or more intricate designs may cost a bit more, but you can usually find something within your budget.

2. Skopelos Cheese and Olive Oil
- Local Markets: Skopelos produces high-quality olive oil and cheese, including the island's famous Skopelos cheese pie (tiropita). You can purchase these products directly from local markets or specialty shops.
- Affordability: A bottle of locally produced olive oil typically costs between €5 and €15, while artisanal cheese can be found for similar prices. These make practical and memorable gifts or keepsakes.

3. Traditional Greek Textiles

- Textile Shops: Look for shops selling handmade textiles, such as embroidered tablecloths, napkins, and cushion covers. These items often feature traditional Greek designs and patterns.
- Affordability: Small textile items like napkins or handkerchiefs can be found for around €10 to €20, while larger items such as tablecloths or throws might range from €25 to €50, depending on the size and intricacy of the design.

4. Local Honey
- Local Honey Producers: Skopelos is known for its delicious honey, often produced by local beekeepers using traditional methods. You can find jars of this sweet treat in local markets and shops.
- Affordability: A jar of local honey typically costs between €5 and €10. It's a sweet and practical souvenir that captures the essence of the island's natural products.

5. Handcrafted Jewelry
- Jewelry Shops: Several local artisans create beautiful handcrafted jewelry, including necklaces, bracelets, and earrings. These pieces often incorporate local materials and traditional designs.
- Affordability: Simple handcrafted jewelry pieces can be found for around €15 to €30. More elaborate designs may cost more, but you can always find something that fits your budget.

6. Greek Spices and Herbs
- Local Markets and Shops: Greek cuisine makes extensive use of herbs and spices. You can purchase dried herbs such as oregano, thyme, and basil, as well as spice blends that are popular in Greek cooking.
- Affordability: Small packets of herbs and spices typically cost between €3 and €8. These make great souvenirs for those who enjoy cooking and want to recreate Greek flavors at home.

7. Handmade Soaps and Skincare Products
- Local Artisan Shops: Look for shops selling handmade soaps and skincare products made from local ingredients like olive oil and herbs. These products often come in attractive packaging and make lovely gifts.
- Affordability: Handmade soaps and skincare products usually range from €5 to €15, depending on the type and size of the item.

8. Wooden Crafts
- Craft Shops: Local artisans often create wooden crafts, including small decorative items like carvings, coasters, and kitchen utensils. These items are often handmade and reflect traditional Greek craftsmanship.

- Affordability: Small wooden items can be found for around €10 to €20, making them affordable and charming souvenirs.

9. Local Art and Paintings
- Art Galleries and Shops: Skopelos has a vibrant art scene, with local artists producing paintings and prints that capture the island's beauty. These can be found in galleries and art shops throughout the island.
- Affordability: Smaller prints and art pieces can be purchased for around €20 to €50, while original paintings may be more expensive. Look for prints or smaller works to stay within budget.

10. Greek Keychains and Magnets
- Souvenir Shops: For a small and inexpensive keepsake, consider purchasing Greek-themed keychains, magnets, or other small trinkets. These are widely available in souvenir shops.
- Affordability: Keychains and magnets typically cost between €3 and €8, making them an easy and budget-friendly option for souvenirs.

11. Traditional Greek Cookbooks
- Bookstores and Shops: Local bookstores and shops often sell Greek cookbooks that feature traditional recipes and cooking techniques. These books make great gifts for food enthusiasts.

- Affordability: Cookbooks are generally priced between €10 and €25, depending on the size and content of the book.

Shopping Tips for Affordable Souvenirs

1. Shop at Local Markets: Visit local markets and artisan fairs for the best deals on handmade crafts and local products. These markets often have lower prices than tourist-oriented shops.

2. Haggle with Vendors: Don't be afraid to negotiate prices, especially in smaller shops and markets. Vendors may be willing to offer discounts if you're purchasing multiple items.

3. Look for Sales and Promotions: Keep an eye out for sales or special promotions, particularly during off-peak times. You might find great deals on souvenirs and local crafts.

4. Buy Directly from Artisans: Purchasing directly from artisans or local producers often means better prices and ensures that you're supporting the local economy.

5. Be Mindful of Fragile Items: If you're purchasing delicate or fragile items, make sure they are packed securely for travel. Consider shipping items home if they are too large or fragile to carry.

By exploring these affordable souvenir options, you can find meaningful and budget-friendly keepsakes that capture the spirit of Skopelos. Whether you're interested in local crafts, traditional foods, or unique gifts, the island offers a range of options that allow you to take home a piece of Greek culture without overspending.

Chapter 3

MOVING AROUND: EXPLORING SKOPELOS

Getting To Skopelos: Ferries And Flights

Skopelos, a beautiful island in the Northern Aegean, is accessible via a combination of flights and ferries. Understanding the best ways to reach Skopelos will help you plan your journey efficiently and make the most of your time on this picturesque island.

1. Ferries to Skopelos
Ferries are the primary mode of transportation to Skopelos, and they offer a scenic and enjoyable journey across the Aegean Sea.

- From Athens to Skopelos

Departure Points: Ferries to Skopelos generally depart from two main ports near Athens: Piraeus and Rafina.

- Piraeus: The main port of Athens, located about 12 km from the city center. It is well-connected by public transport, including metro and bus services.
- Rafina: Located about 30 km from central Athens. Rafina is also accessible by bus and car, and it can be a convenient option if you are traveling from the northern suburbs or the airport.

Ferry Operators: Several ferry companies operate routes to Skopelos, including:
- Hellenic Seaways: Offers high-speed and conventional ferries to Skopelos. The journey typically takes around 1.5 to 2 hours by high-speed ferry and 4 to 5 hours by conventional ferry.
- Blue Star Ferries: Provides conventional ferry services to Skopelos, usually involving a transfer at the nearby island of Skiathos. Travel times can vary, but expect around 4 to 6 hours, including the transfer.

Ticket Booking: Ferries can be booked online through the ferry companies' websites or through third-party booking platforms. It is advisable to book tickets in advance, especially during peak travel seasons.

- From Thessaloniki to Skopelos

Departure Point: Ferries to Skopelos from Thessaloniki usually depart from the port of Thessaloniki.

Ferry Operators:
- Hellenic Seaways: Operates routes from Thessaloniki to Skopelos, often with a transfer at Skiathos. The journey can take approximately 4 to 6 hours, including the transfer time.

Ticket Booking: Tickets can be purchased online or at the Thessaloniki port. As with routes from Athens, it is recommended to book in advance.

2. Flights to Skopelos

Skopelos does not have its own airport, so flights are typically routed through nearby islands or the mainland.

- To Skiathos Airport (JSI)
- Main Option: The closest airport to Skopelos is Skiathos International Airport. It is located on the island of Skiathos, which is just a short ferry ride away from Skopelos.
- Flights: Skiathos Airport receives flights from Athens (ATH) and other major Greek cities, as well

as some international destinations, particularly during the summer months.
 - Transfer to Skopelos: From Skiathos, you can take a ferry to Skopelos. Ferries from Skiathos to Skopelos typically take around 30 minutes to 1 hour.

- To Volos Airport (VOL)
 - Alternative Option: Volos Airport is another option, though it is farther from Skopelos compared to Skiathos.
 - Flights: Volos Airport has flights mainly from Athens, with occasional seasonal flights from other Greek cities.
 - Transfer to Skopelos: From Volos, you can take a ferry to Skopelos. The ferry ride from Volos to Skopelos generally takes around 2 to 3 hours.

3. Getting from the Airport to the Ferry Ports
- From Athens Airport (ATH)
 - To Piraeus: You can take a taxi, shuttle bus, or metro (Line 1) to Piraeus port. The journey takes approximately 45 minutes to 1 hour.
 - To Rafina: Taxis and shuttle buses are available to Rafina port. The trip takes about 30 to 40 minutes.

- From Skiathos Airport (JSI)

- To Skiathos Port: A short taxi ride or local bus can get you from the airport to Skiathos port, where you can catch a ferry to Skopelos.

- From Volos Airport (VOL)
  - To Volos Port: A taxi or local bus will transport you from the airport to the port in Volos, where ferries to Skopelos are available.

4. Tips for Traveling to Skopelos
- Book Early: During peak travel seasons, such as summer, both flights and ferries can get fully booked. Make reservations well in advance to secure your travel arrangements.
- Check Schedules: Ferry and flight schedules can vary depending on the season and weather conditions. Check schedules and possible changes before your trip.
- Travel Insurance: Consider purchasing travel insurance that covers transportation delays or cancellations, especially if you have tight connections between flights and ferries.
- Luggage: Be aware of luggage policies for both flights and ferries. Ferries typically have more lenient luggage allowances, but it's still good to check in advance.

By understanding your options for ferries and flights, you can plan a smooth and enjoyable journey to Skopelos, ensuring that you arrive ready to explore the island's stunning landscapes and vibrant culture.

Navigating The Island: Car Rentals And Public Transport

Skopelos, with its charming villages, scenic landscapes, and numerous beaches, is best explored with some form of transportation. While the island offers several options for getting around, including car rentals and public transport, each has its advantages depending on your travel style and itinerary.

1. Car Rentals

Renting a car is one of the most convenient ways to explore Skopelos, allowing you to reach more remote areas and travel at your own pace.

- Rental Agencies
 - Local Agencies: Skopelos has several local car rental agencies offering a range of vehicles from small cars to larger SUVs. Examples include Skopelos Rent a Car and Skopelos Auto Rentals. These agencies often provide competitive rates and personalized service.
 - International Agencies: If you prefer, you can also find international car rental companies with

offices in nearby towns or at the airports on Skiathos or Volos, where you can arrange for a car to be ready when you arrive.

- Booking Tips
 - Advance Booking: It's advisable to book your rental car in advance, especially during peak tourist seasons, to ensure availability and secure the best rates.
 - Online Reservations: Use online booking platforms to compare prices and read reviews. Booking in advance can often result in better deals compared to renting upon arrival.

- Driving in Skopelos
 - Road Conditions: Skopelos has a mix of paved and unpaved roads. While main roads are generally well-maintained, some of the smaller, rural roads may be narrow and winding.
 - Parking: Parking in Skopelos Town can be challenging during busy times. Look for designated parking areas and be mindful of local parking regulations. In the villages and more remote areas, parking is usually less of an issue.

- Car Rental Requirements
 - License: A valid driver's license is required, and an International Driving Permit (IDP) may be

necessary if your license is not in the Latin alphabet.

- Insurance: Check that your rental includes adequate insurance coverage, and consider purchasing additional insurance for peace of mind.

2. Public Transport

Skopelos offers various public transport options that can be both economical and convenient for getting around the island.

- Buses
  - Local Bus Service: The local bus network, operated by Skopelos Bus Service, connects major towns, villages, and popular beaches. Buses run regularly but may have limited schedules, especially in the off-season.
  - Routes and Timetables: Bus routes typically cover key locations including Skopelos Town, Glossa, and popular beaches like Kastani and Panormos. Timetables can vary, so it's a good idea to check the schedule in advance or ask at your accommodation for the latest information.

- Taxis
  - Availability: Taxis are available throughout Skopelos and can be a convenient option for shorter trips or when public transport is not running. Taxis can be hailed on the street or booked by phone.

- Cost: Taxi fares are generally reasonable, but rates can vary depending on the distance and time of day. It's a good idea to confirm the fare before starting your journey.

- Boat Taxis
  - Water Transport: Boat taxis provide a unique way to travel between Skopelos and nearby islands or secluded beaches. These are particularly useful for reaching places that are not easily accessible by land.
  - Booking: Boat taxis can usually be arranged through local tour operators or directly with the service providers. Prices can vary based on the destination and the number of passengers.

- Bicycles and Scooters
  - Rental Options: For a more leisurely mode of transport, you can rent bicycles or scooters from local rental shops. This option is ideal for exploring nearby areas and enjoying the island's scenic routes.
  - Safety: Ensure you wear a helmet and follow local traffic regulations. Roads can be hilly and winding, so be prepared for a bit of a workout if you choose to bike.

- Walking
  - Exploring on Foot: Skopelos Town and many of the island's villages are charming and walkable,

with narrow streets and picturesque scenery. Walking can be a pleasant way to explore local shops, restaurants, and attractions.

 - Hiking Trails: Skopelos has several hiking trails that offer stunning views and a chance to experience the island's natural beauty. Trails vary in difficulty, so choose one that suits your fitness level and interests.

3. Tips for Getting Around

- Plan Your Itinerary: Whether you're using public transport or renting a car, plan your itinerary in advance to make the most of your time on the island. Consider the locations you want to visit and the best modes of transport to reach them.

- Check Schedules and Routes: Public transport schedules and routes can change, so it's important to stay informed about the latest information. Ask for updates at your accommodation or check online resources.

- Be Prepared for Varied Conditions: Skopelos' terrain can be diverse, with both coastal roads and mountainous areas. If you're renting a car, choose a vehicle suitable for the conditions you'll encounter.

By choosing the right mode of transportation and planning your travel routes, you can navigate Skopelos with ease and fully enjoy everything this beautiful island has to offer.

Scenic Walks And Cycling Routes

Skopelos, known for its lush landscapes and picturesque coastline, offers numerous scenic walks and cycling routes for those who prefer to explore the island at a slower pace. Whether you're interested in hiking through ancient forests or cycling along coastal paths, Skopelos provides a range of outdoor activities to suit various interests and fitness levels.

Scenic Walks

1. Skopelos Town to Loutraki
   - Route: This coastal walk takes you from Skopelos Town to the charming village of Loutraki. The route follows the shoreline and provides stunning views of the Aegean Sea and nearby islands.
   - Distance: Approximately 10 km (6 miles) one way.
   - Duration: About 3 to 4 hours.
   - Highlights: Enjoy the beautiful coastal scenery, small beaches, and traditional Greek architecture in Loutraki. The path also passes through pine forests and offers panoramic views.

2. The Skopelos Olive Grove Walk

- Route: Explore the olive groves surrounding Skopelos Town. This walk takes you through lush groves, ancient olive trees, and traditional farms.
  - Distance: Approximately 5 km (3 miles) loop.
  - Duration: About 1.5 to 2 hours.
  - Highlights: Discover the island's agricultural heritage, enjoy the peaceful rural landscape, and experience local flora. This walk is particularly pleasant in the spring when the groves are in full bloom.

3. Panormos Beach to Agios Ioannis Kastri
  - Route: This trail leads from Panormos Beach to the iconic Agios Ioannis Kastri, a church perched on a rock outcrop.
  - Distance: Approximately 8 km (5 miles) round trip.
  - Duration: About 2 to 3 hours.
  - Highlights: Enjoy scenic coastal views, the beautiful beach at Panormos, and the dramatic setting of Agios Ioannis Kastri. The trail offers opportunities for swimming and photography along the way.

4. The Old Monastery Trail
  - Route: This route connects several historic monasteries in the interior of the island. It includes trails through dense forests and past ancient stone structures.

- Distance: Approximately 12 km (7.5 miles) loop.
- Duration: About 3 to 4 hours.
- Highlights: Visit historic monasteries like Moni Evangelistria and Moni Sotiros, and enjoy the serene atmosphere of the island's interior.

5. Glossa to Kastro
- Route: This walk connects the village of Glossa with the ancient fortress of Kastro. It includes both coastal and inland paths, offering diverse scenery.
- Distance: Approximately 7 km (4.5 miles) one way.
- Duration: About 2 to 3 hours.
- Highlights: Explore the charming village of Glossa, enjoy sweeping views from the fortress, and discover historical ruins.

Cycling Routes
1. Skopelos Town to Glysteri Beach
- Route: This popular cycling route takes you from Skopelos Town to Glysteri Beach, following a combination of coastal and forest paths.
- Distance: Approximately 8 km (5 miles) one way.
- Duration: About 1.5 hours.
- Highlights: Enjoy scenic coastal views, lush forest areas, and the tranquil beach of Glysteri. The

route is suitable for moderate cyclists and offers a rewarding beach destination.

2. The Central Island Loop
- Route: This loop route takes you through the heart of the island, covering various villages, including Skopelos Town, Glossa, and the surrounding countryside.
- Distance: Approximately 20 km (12.5 miles).
- Duration: About 2 to 3 hours.
- Highlights: Experience the diverse landscapes of Skopelos, including rolling hills, olive groves, and charming villages. This route provides a comprehensive overview of the island's interior.

3. Agios Konstantinos to Panormos
- Route: Cycle from the village of Agios Konstantinos to Panormos Beach, passing through scenic countryside and coastal areas.
- Distance: Approximately 12 km (7.5 miles) one way.
- Duration: About 1.5 to 2 hours.
- Highlights: Enjoy the varied terrain, including picturesque rural landscapes and coastal views. Panormos Beach is a great spot to relax after your ride.

4. The Southern Coastal Route

- Route: This route follows the southern coast of Skopelos, passing through several beaches and coastal villages.
- Distance: Approximately 15 km (9 miles) round trip.
- Duration: About 2 hours.
- Highlights: Explore beautiful beaches, such as Stafilos and Velanio, and enjoy stunning coastal views. This route is ideal for those looking to combine cycling with beach visits.

5. Kastro to Agios Ioannis Kastri
- Route: This challenging route takes you from the ancient fortress of Kastro to the church of Agios Ioannis Kastri, covering both coastal and hilly terrain.
- Distance: Approximately 10 km (6 miles) one way.
- Duration: About 2 hours.
- Highlights: Experience dramatic coastal views, steep climbs, and the unique setting of Agios Ioannis Kastri. This route is suited for more experienced cyclists seeking a rewarding ride.

Tips for Scenic Walks and Cycling
- Plan Ahead: Research and plan your routes in advance. Check maps and guidebooks to ensure you're aware of the terrain, distance, and difficulty level.

- Bring Essentials: Carry essentials such as water, snacks, sunscreen, a hat, and a map or GPS device. Proper footwear is crucial for walking, and a helmet is recommended for cycling.
- Check Weather Conditions: Weather can change quickly, so check the forecast before setting out. Avoid walking or cycling in extreme heat or rain.
- Respect Local Wildlife and Environment: Stick to marked trails, avoid disturbing wildlife, and dispose of waste properly. This helps preserve the island's natural beauty.
- Safety First: If you're unfamiliar with the area, consider joining a guided tour for a safe and informative experience. Inform someone about your plans if venturing into remote areas.

By exploring Skopelos on foot or by bike, you'll experience the island's stunning natural beauty up close and enjoy a more immersive travel experience. Whether you choose a leisurely coastal walk or a more challenging cycling route, Skopelos offers plenty of opportunities for outdoor adventure.

Boat Trips: Island Hopping And Coastal Cruises

Skopelos, nestled in the Northern Aegean, offers a fantastic base for exploring nearby islands and enjoying the stunning coastline. Boat trips, including island hopping and coastal cruises, are an excellent way to experience the natural beauty and cultural richness of the region.

Island Hopping

Island hopping around Skopelos allows you to discover the unique charm of neighboring islands, each with its own distinct character and attractions.

- Skiathos
 - Overview: Skiathos, the closest island to Skopelos, is known for its vibrant nightlife, beautiful beaches, and lively town. It's a popular destination for day trips from Skopelos.

- How to Get There: Ferries run regularly between Skopelos and Skiathos, with a journey time of about 30 minutes to 1 hour. You can also use water taxis for a more personalized trip.
  - Highlights: Visit the famous Koukounaries Beach, explore the charming town of Skiathos, and enjoy a range of dining and shopping options.

- Alonissos
  - Overview: Alonissos is renowned for its natural beauty and the nearby Marine Park, which protects a variety of marine life, including the Mediterranean monk seal.
  - How to Get There: Ferries from Skopelos to Alonissos typically take about 1 to 1.5 hours. Routes may include stops at other islands, such as Peristera.
  - Highlights: Explore the picturesque village of Patitiri, hike through lush landscapes, and visit the Marine Park for wildlife spotting and nature walks.

- Skyros
  - Overview: Skyros is a more distant island known for its traditional Greek charm, unique local crafts, and beautiful landscapes.
  - How to Get There: Ferries to Skyros are less frequent and may require a transfer at other islands or mainland ports. The journey can take around 2 to 3 hours.

- Highlights: Discover the quaint town of Skyros, explore ancient ruins, and enjoy the island's distinctive blend of traditional and modern Greek culture.

- Pelion Peninsula (Mainland)
  - Overview: While not an island, the Pelion Peninsula offers a fascinating alternative with its mix of mountains, beaches, and charming villages.
  - How to Get There: Ferries from Skopelos to the mainland ports of Volos or Kymi, followed by a drive to the Pelion Peninsula, are common.
  - Highlights: Visit the scenic villages of Portaria and Makrinitsa, enjoy the beautiful beaches, and explore the lush landscapes of the peninsula.

Coastal Cruises

Coastal cruises provide a relaxing way to explore Skopelos' coastline and enjoy the island's natural beauty from the sea. These cruises can range from short excursions to full-day or multi-day trips.

- Half-Day Coastal Cruises
  - Overview: These shorter cruises typically focus on the southern or northern coast of Skopelos, providing a glimpse of the island's stunning scenery and hidden beaches.

- Itineraries: Common routes include visits to beaches like Stafilos, Velanio, and Agnondas, as well as stops at picturesque coves and bays.
  - Activities: Enjoy swimming and snorkeling in crystal-clear waters, relax on deck, and take in the views of the island's rugged coastline.

- **Full-Day Coastal Cruises**
  - Overview: Full-day cruises offer a more comprehensive exploration of Skopelos and surrounding islands, often including stops for swimming, dining, and sightseeing.
  - Itineraries: Typical routes may include stops at popular beaches, remote coves, and neighboring islands such as Alonissos or Skiathos.
  - Activities: Activities may include guided tours, beach stops, BBQ lunches, and opportunities to explore local attractions. Some cruises may offer themed experiences, such as traditional Greek music or dance.

- **Private Yacht Charters**
  - Overview: For a more personalized experience, consider renting a private yacht or boat. This option allows for flexible itineraries and customized experiences.
  - Charter Options: Choose from a range of yacht sizes and types, from small sailing boats to luxury

motor yachts. Many companies offer half-day, full-day, or multi-day charters.
- Highlights: Enjoy a bespoke itinerary, including stops at secluded beaches, fishing spots, or other islands. Chartering a yacht provides a high level of comfort and privacy.

- **Sunset Cruises**
- Overview: Sunset cruises offer a romantic and picturesque way to experience the beauty of Skopelos' coastline as the sun sets over the Aegean Sea.
- Itineraries: These cruises typically depart in the late afternoon and return after sunset. They often include leisurely cruising along the coast, with a focus on enjoying the sunset views.
- Activities: Relax on deck, enjoy a drink or dinner (if included), and take in the breathtaking views of the sunset over the water.

Booking Tips
- Advance Reservations: Book your island hopping trips and coastal cruises in advance, especially during peak travel seasons. Popular excursions can fill up quickly.
- Check Reviews: Read reviews and compare options to ensure you choose reputable tour operators with good service and safety records.

- Consider the Weather: Check the weather forecast before booking or embarking on boat trips. Conditions can affect the comfort and safety of your journey.
- Bring Essentials: Pack essentials such as sunscreen, a hat, swimwear, a camera, and a light jacket for cooler evenings. For longer trips, bring snacks and water.

Safety and Environmental Tips
- Safety First: Always wear a life jacket when on a boat, and follow the crew's safety instructions. Ensure that the boat you choose meets safety regulations.
- Respect Marine Life: Avoid disturbing wildlife, including marine animals. Follow guidelines set by the Marine Park or tour operators.
- Protect the Environment: Dispose of waste properly and avoid leaving litter behind. Be mindful of your impact on the natural environment.

By exploring Skopelos and its neighboring islands through island hopping and coastal cruises, you'll experience the region's natural beauty, cultural heritage, and diverse landscapes from a unique perspective. Whether you opt for a leisurely coastal cruise or an adventurous island-hopping journey, the waters around Skopelos offer memorable and enriching travel experiences.

Chapter 4

SLEEPING OVER: WHERE TO STAY

Top Hotels For Every Budgets

Skopelos offers a wide range of accommodation options to suit every budget and preference. Whether you're looking for luxury, mid-range comfort, or budget-friendly stays, there's a perfect place for you to rest and recharge.

Luxury Hotels
1. Skopelos Grand Hotel
   - Overview: A five-star hotel offering a blend of modern luxury and traditional Greek charm.

Located near Skopelos Town, it provides stunning views of the Aegean Sea and lush surroundings.
 - Features: Elegant rooms and suites, an outdoor pool, a spa and wellness center, fine dining restaurant, and direct beach access.
 - Price Range: $200 - $350 per night.

2. Hotel Skiathos Princess
 - Overview: Situated on the neighboring island of Skiathos, this luxury hotel is perfect for those looking for a high-end experience with easy access to Skopelos via a short ferry ride.
 - Features: Spacious rooms, multiple dining options, a private beach, an outdoor pool, and a spa.
 - Price Range: $250 - $400 per night.

3. Agnanti Hotel
 - Overview: Located on a hill with panoramic views of Skopelos Town and the sea, this boutique hotel offers a blend of luxury and tranquility.
 - Features: Stylish rooms, an infinity pool, gourmet restaurant, and personalized service.
 - Price Range: $150 - $250 per night.

Mid-Range Hotels

1. Hotel Dionysos
 - Overview: A comfortable and well-rated hotel in Skopelos Town, offering easy access to local attractions and the port.

- Features: Modern rooms, a pool, breakfast service, and friendly staff.
- Price Range: $80 - $130 per night.

2. Skopelos Village Hotel
- Overview: Located a short walk from Skopelos Town, this hotel offers a mix of traditional Greek architecture and modern amenities.
- Features: Comfortable rooms, an outdoor pool, garden areas, and a breakfast buffet.
- Price Range: $90 - $140 per night.

3. Villa Melina
- Overview: Set in a peaceful location near Skopelos Town, this family-run hotel offers a relaxed atmosphere with beautiful gardens.
- Features: Clean rooms, a pool, complimentary breakfast, and a warm, welcoming atmosphere.
- Price Range: $70 - $120 per night.

Budget Hotels

1. Hotel Asterias
- Overview: A budget-friendly option in Skopelos Town, ideal for travelers looking for basic amenities and great value.
- Features: Simple and clean rooms, a small pool, and easy access to the town center.
- Price Range: $50 - $80 per night.

2. Pension Anna
- Overview: Located in a central position in Skopelos Town, this pension offers affordable and comfortable accommodation.
- Features: Basic rooms, a communal area, and proximity to local shops and restaurants.
- Price Range: $40 - $70 per night.

3. Margarita Hotel
- Overview: A charming and economical choice, situated in a quiet area but within walking distance of Skopelos Town.
- Features: Simple rooms, a small garden, and a friendly atmosphere.
- Price Range: $35 - $60 per night.

Unique Stays

1. Paliokastro Suites
- Overview: For a unique experience, these suites offer a blend of modern comfort and traditional Greek architecture, set in a picturesque location.
- Features: Private suites with sea views, a garden, and personalized service.
- Price Range: $120 - $180 per night.

2. Charming Villas
- Overview: Several charming villas are available for rent on Skopelos, providing a more private and

home-like stay with options for various sizes and amenities.

- Features: Private pools, gardens, and fully equipped kitchens.

- Price Range: $150 - $300 per night, depending on size and location.

Booking Tips

- Book Early: Skopelos is a popular destination, especially during peak travel seasons. Booking in advance will help secure the best rates and availability.

- Check Reviews: Read reviews on booking platforms to get a sense of the hotel's quality and the experiences of previous guests.

- Consider Location: Think about what you want to be close to—whether it's the beach, local attractions, or the town center—when choosing your accommodation.

- Look for Deals: Keep an eye out for special offers, discounts, or packages that may include additional perks like meals or activities.

With these options, you can find the perfect place to stay in Skopelos, whether you're seeking luxury, comfort, or budget-friendly accommodations. Enjoy your stay on this beautiful island!

Charming Villas And Cozy Guesthouses

For travelers seeking a more intimate and personalized experience on Skopelos, charming villas and cozy guesthouses offer the perfect blend of comfort, style, and local character.

Charming Villas

1. Villa Eleni
   - Overview: Nestled in a serene location with panoramic views of the Aegean Sea, Villa Eleni offers a luxurious and private stay.
   - Features: The villa includes multiple bedrooms, a private pool, a fully equipped kitchen, and spacious outdoor areas with stunning sea views.
   - Price Range: $200 - $350 per night.
   - Highlights: Ideal for families or groups looking for privacy and comfort. The villa is well-situated for exploring nearby beaches and local attractions.

2. Villa Amalia
   - Overview: This beautifully designed villa combines traditional Greek architecture with modern amenities, set amidst lush gardens.
   - Features: Includes private terraces, a swimming pool, and stylish interiors with high-quality furnishings.
   - Price Range: $180 - $300 per night.
   - Highlights: Offers a tranquil retreat with easy access to Skopelos Town and nearby beaches. Perfect for a relaxing getaway with a touch of elegance.

3. Villa Meli
   - Overview: A charming and cozy villa located in a picturesque setting with beautiful views of the island's rolling hills.
   - Features: Features include a private pool, well-maintained gardens, and a modern kitchen. The villa offers a comfortable and homey atmosphere.
   - Price Range: $150 - $250 per night.
   - Highlights: Ideal for couples or small families seeking a peaceful escape while still being close to local amenities and attractions.

4. Villa Nereus
   - Overview: A luxurious villa with direct access to the beach and stunning sea views, Villa Nereus offers a blend of sophistication and natural beauty.

- Features: Includes spacious living areas, multiple bedrooms, a private beach area, and outdoor dining options.
- Price Range: $250 - $400 per night.
- Highlights: Perfect for those wanting to combine beachside relaxation with high-end comfort. The villa's exclusive location ensures a memorable stay.

Cozy Guesthouses

1. Pension Katerina
- Overview: A family-run guesthouse in Skopelos Town offering a warm and welcoming atmosphere with personalized service.
- Features: Simple yet comfortable rooms, a communal terrace, and a cozy lounge area. Breakfast is often included.
- Price Range: $60 - $90 per night.
- Highlights: Close to local shops and restaurants, providing easy access to the town's amenities while offering a homely feel.

2. Guesthouse Ilias
- Overview: Located near Skopelos Town, this guesthouse offers traditional Greek hospitality and a relaxing environment.
- Features: Comfortable rooms, a beautiful garden, and a communal kitchen. The guesthouse is known for its friendly and attentive service.
- Price Range: $50 - $80 per night.

- Highlights: Provides a great balance of comfort and value. Ideal for travelers looking for a peaceful stay with easy access to local attractions.

3. Pension Yiannis
   - Overview: Situated in a quiet area of Skopelos Town, Pension Yiannis offers charming and affordable accommodations.
   - Features: Features include well-maintained rooms, a small garden, and a friendly atmosphere. Breakfast options are available.
   - Price Range: $40 - $70 per night.
   - Highlights: Offers a great base for exploring Skopelos Town and is known for its cleanliness and hospitable owners.

4. Katerina's Guesthouse
   - Overview: A cozy guesthouse located slightly outside of Skopelos Town, providing a peaceful retreat with easy access to local amenities.
   - Features: Includes comfortable rooms, a communal area, and a garden. The guesthouse offers a homely and relaxed environment.
   - Price Range: $55 - $85 per night.
   - Highlights: Ideal for travelers looking for a tranquil setting with the convenience of being close to the town center.

Local Experiences

- Traditional Greek Breakfast: Many guesthouses offer a traditional Greek breakfast, which can be a delightful way to start your day.
- Personalized Service: Smaller guesthouses often provide a more personalized experience, with owners who can offer local tips and recommendations.
- Private Pool and Gardens: Villas with private pools and gardens provide a luxurious and secluded experience, perfect for relaxation and privacy.

Staying in a charming villa or cozy guesthouse in Skopelos offers a unique and memorable experience, allowing you to enjoy the island's natural beauty and warm hospitality. Whether you're looking for luxury, comfort, or a budget-friendly option, Skopelos has a variety of accommodations to suit every traveler's needs.

Unique Stays: Traditional Homes And Eco-lodges

Skopelos offers a range of unique accommodation options that blend traditional Greek charm with modern sustainability. Staying in traditional homes or eco-lodges provides a distinctive experience that immerses you in the island's culture and natural beauty.

Traditional Homes
1. The Skopelos House
   - Overview: A beautifully restored traditional home located in Skopelos Town, offering a blend of historic charm and modern comforts.
   - Features: Includes traditional stonework, wooden beams, and tiled floors, with modern amenities like Wi-Fi and air conditioning. The

house features a private courtyard and is decorated with local art and antiques.
 - Price Range: $120 - $200 per night.
 - Highlights: Experience authentic Greek architecture and decor, and enjoy easy access to local shops and restaurants.

2. Villa Kastro
 - Overview: Located near the ancient fortress of Kastro, this traditional villa offers stunning views and historic charm.
 - Features: Traditional design with stone walls and wooden ceilings, a private garden, and a large terrace. The villa is furnished with antique pieces and offers modern conveniences.
 - Price Range: $150 - $250 per night.
 - Highlights: Ideal for history enthusiasts and those looking to immerse themselves in traditional Greek culture. The location offers panoramic views and a quiet retreat.

3. The Old Stone House
 - Overview: This traditional stone house is set in a scenic location, combining rustic charm with comfort.
 - Features: Features include a stone fireplace, traditional Greek furnishings, a well-equipped kitchen, and a private terrace. The house is surrounded by lush gardens.

- Price Range: $100 - $180 per night.
  - Highlights: Enjoy a cozy and authentic Greek experience in a beautifully preserved traditional setting.

4. Archontiko Skopelos
  - Overview: A historical residence that has been converted into a charming guesthouse, offering a glimpse into traditional Skopelos life.
  - Features: Traditional architectural elements, antique furnishings, and modern amenities. The guesthouse includes a shared garden and communal areas.
  - Price Range: $80 - $130 per night.
  - Highlights: Experience a blend of historical elegance and modern comfort, with a focus on preserving the local heritage.

Eco-Lodges
1. Eco-Lodge Agnontas
  - Overview: Set in the coastal village of Agnontas, this eco-lodge emphasizes sustainability and harmony with nature.
  - Features: Includes eco-friendly amenities, such as solar-powered energy, water-saving fixtures, and organic products. The lodge offers comfortable rooms with natural materials and beautiful sea views.
  - Price Range: $100 - $160 per night.

- Highlights: Enjoy a sustainable stay with a focus on environmental conservation and local organic produce.

2. Green Retreat Skopelos
 - Overview: An eco-friendly retreat located in a secluded area of Skopelos, designed to blend seamlessly with the natural surroundings.
 - Features: Offers accommodations in eco-friendly cabins with energy-efficient systems, rainwater harvesting, and organic gardens. The retreat promotes eco-conscious living and provides a peaceful escape.
 - Price Range: $120 - $180 per night.
 - Highlights: Experience a green lifestyle in a tranquil setting, with opportunities for eco-tourism and nature activities.

3. Eco-Village Skopelos
 - Overview: A small eco-village offering traditional Greek-style lodgings with a focus on environmental sustainability and community living.
 - Features: Includes eco-lodges built with natural materials, a communal garden, and solar energy systems. The village promotes sustainable practices and offers a unique cultural experience.
 - Price Range: $90 - $150 per night.

- Highlights: Enjoy an immersive eco-friendly experience with opportunities to engage in local community activities and sustainability workshops.

4. Organic Farm Stay
   - Overview: Situated on an organic farm, this eco-lodge offers a unique stay with a focus on sustainable agriculture and local produce.
   - Features: Includes cozy lodgings with eco-friendly amenities, access to the farm's organic produce, and opportunities for farm tours and activities.
   - Price Range: $80 - $130 per night.
   - Highlights: Experience farm life, enjoy fresh organic meals, and learn about sustainable farming practices.

Local Experiences
- Cultural Immersion: Staying in a traditional home provides a unique opportunity to immerse yourself in the local culture and history of Skopelos.
- Sustainable Living: Eco-lodges offer a chance to experience a more sustainable lifestyle and participate in activities that promote environmental conservation.
- Local Cuisine: Many eco-lodges and traditional homes feature local and organic produce, providing an authentic taste of Greek cuisine.

By choosing a traditional home or eco-lodge in Skopelos, you'll enjoy a distinctive and enriching stay that reflects the island's heritage and commitment to sustainability. These unique accommodations offer memorable experiences that go beyond conventional lodging, making your visit to Skopelos truly special.

Best Areas To Stay: Town, Beach Or Countryside?

Skopelos offers a variety of areas to stay, each providing a unique experience depending on whether you prefer the vibrancy of the town, the tranquility of the beach, or the serenity of the countryside.

1. Skopelos Town
Overview: Skopelos Town is the island's bustling hub, rich in history and culture. It's ideal for those who want to be in the heart of the action, close to restaurants, shops, and historical sites.

- Accommodation Options:
  - Hotels: Choose from a range of hotels, from budget-friendly options to luxurious stays. Many hotels offer easy access to the town's main attractions.

- Guesthouses: Cozy and family-run guesthouses provide a more intimate and personalized experience.
- Apartments: For longer stays or a home-like atmosphere, consider renting an apartment in the town.

- Highlights:
  - Historic Sites: Explore the charming old town, visit the 19th-century church of Agios Nikolaos, and wander through narrow, winding streets.
  - Dining and Shopping: Enjoy a variety of restaurants, cafes, and shops offering local products and souvenirs.
  - Accessibility: Easy access to the port and public transport options for exploring the rest of the island.

- Best For: Travelers who want convenience, cultural experiences, and a lively atmosphere.

2. Beach Areas
Overview: Skopelos is renowned for its beautiful beaches, which offer a more relaxed and scenic stay. Staying near the beach provides easy access to sunbathing, swimming, and seaside dining.

- Agnondas Beach

- Overview: A picturesque beach with clear waters and a laid-back atmosphere, perfect for a tranquil stay.
  - Accommodation Options: Beachfront hotels, cozy guesthouses, and self-catering apartments.
  - Highlights: Lovely beach bars and restaurants, easy access to water activities, and stunning sunset views.

- Stafilos Beach
  - Overview: A popular sandy beach surrounded by lush greenery, offering a more vibrant beach experience.
  - Accommodation Options: Nearby hotels and villas with easy access to the beach.
  - Highlights: Great for swimming and sunbathing, with nearby cafes and snack bars.

- Panormos Beach
  - Overview: Known for its clear blue waters and relaxed vibe, Panormos is ideal for those seeking a peaceful beach retreat.
  - Accommodation Options: Beachfront resorts, charming guesthouses, and villas with sea views.
  - Highlights: Beautiful beachside dining options, calm waters, and stunning natural scenery.

- Best For: Beach lovers who enjoy immediate access to the sea, water sports, and coastal dining.

3. Countryside
Overview: The Skopelos countryside offers a serene escape from the more tourist-heavy areas. It's perfect for those looking to experience the island's natural beauty and traditional way of life.

- Glossa Village
  - Overview: A charming village in the northern part of the island, known for its traditional architecture and stunning views.
  - Accommodation Options: Traditional guesthouses, eco-lodges, and rustic villas.
  - Highlights: Explore traditional Greek villages, enjoy panoramic views, and visit local tavernas.

- Kastani Beach Area
  - Overview: Located near the famous Kastani Beach, this area combines beautiful coastal views with a rural setting.
  - Accommodation Options: Villas and guesthouses offering privacy and proximity to both the beach and countryside.
  - Highlights: Access to the renowned Kastani Beach, picturesque surroundings, and quiet relaxation.

- Patitiri Area (Alonissos)

- Overview: Though technically on the neighboring island of Alonissos, Patitiri provides a lovely countryside experience with access to natural parks and tranquil settings.
- Accommodation Options: Eco-lodges and traditional guesthouses with easy access to nature.
- Highlights: Explore the Alonissos Marine Park, enjoy hiking and nature walks, and experience a quieter island atmosphere.

- Best For: Travelers seeking tranquility, nature lovers, and those interested in traditional Greek life.

Booking Tips
- Consider Your Preferences: Think about what you want from your stay—whether it's the convenience of the town, the relaxation of the beach, or the peace of the countryside.
- Check Accessibility: Ensure that your chosen area has good transport links, especially if you plan to explore different parts of the island.
- Look for Deals: Keep an eye out for special offers or packages that may include additional perks or discounts.

Local Experiences
- Town: Engage in local festivals, enjoy traditional Greek music, and explore historic sites.

- Beach: Relax on sandy shores, participate in water sports, and savor fresh seafood at beachside restaurants.

- Countryside: Discover traditional villages, enjoy scenic hikes, and experience the island's rural charm.

By choosing the right area to stay in Skopelos, you can tailor your experience to fit your preferences and make the most of your visit to this beautiful island. Whether you choose the bustling town, serene beaches, or tranquil countryside, Skopelos offers a range of accommodations to suit every traveler's needs.

Chapter 5

EATING: SAVORING THE FLAVORS OF SKOPELOS

Traditional Skopelos Dishes You Must Try

Skopelos, known for its lush landscapes and picturesque views, also boasts a rich culinary heritage that reflects the island's Greek traditions. From fresh seafood to hearty local dishes, the cuisine of Skopelos is a delightful journey for the taste buds.

1. Skopelitiki Cheese Pie (Skopelos Tiropita)

- Description: A local variation of the traditional Greek tiropita, this savory pie is made with a generous amount of Skopelos cheese, which is renowned for its rich flavor and crumbly texture.
- Ingredients: Skopelos cheese (a type of local feta), eggs, olive oil, and phyllo dough.
- Taste: The pie has a creamy, tangy filling encased in a crisp, flaky crust. It's often enjoyed as a snack or a light meal.
- Where to Try: Many local bakeries and tavernas serve this dish, with some family-owned places offering secret recipes that have been passed down through generations.

2. Stuffed Zucchini Flowers (Koukia Gemista)
- Description: This dish features zucchini flowers stuffed with a mixture of rice, herbs, and sometimes minced meat, then cooked in a tomato sauce.
- Ingredients: Zucchini flowers, rice, onions, dill, mint, tomatoes, and olive oil.
- Taste: The stuffed flowers have a delicate flavor, with the rice and herbs creating a savory, aromatic filling that pairs beautifully with the tangy tomato sauce.
- Where to Try: Look for this dish in local restaurants and family-run eateries, especially those that focus on traditional Greek vegetarian cuisine.

3. Grilled Octopus (Octapodi Sti Skara)

- Description: A staple of Greek coastal cuisine, this dish features octopus that's marinated and then grilled to perfection.
- Ingredients: Fresh octopus, olive oil, lemon juice, garlic, and herbs like oregano.
- Taste: The grilled octopus is tender and smoky, with a subtle char and a fresh, tangy flavor from the lemon and herbs.
- Where to Try: Available at seafood restaurants and tavernas along the coast of Skopelos, where the octopus is often freshly caught.

4. Lamb with Artichokes (Arni me Anginares)
- Description: A hearty dish featuring tender lamb cooked with artichokes in a flavorful, often lemon-infused sauce.
- Ingredients: Lamb, artichokes, onions, garlic, lemon, olive oil, and various herbs.
- Taste: The dish combines the rich flavor of lamb with the tender, slightly tangy artichokes, creating a comforting and satisfying meal.
- Where to Try: This dish is commonly found in traditional Greek tavernas and is a favorite for special family meals.

5. Greek Salad (Horiatiki Salata)
- Description: A refreshing and simple salad made with fresh vegetables, feta cheese, and olives, typically dressed with olive oil and herbs.

- Ingredients: Tomatoes, cucumbers, red onions, green peppers, olives, feta cheese, olive oil, and oregano.
- Taste: Crisp and refreshing, with the creamy feta and tangy olives adding depth to the fresh vegetables.
- Where to Try: Found in almost every restaurant and tavern in Skopelos, often enjoyed as a side dish or light meal.

6. Skopelos Style Souvlaki
- Description: Skopelos puts its unique spin on this Greek classic by marinating the meat in a blend of local spices and herbs before grilling.
- Ingredients: Pork or chicken, olive oil, garlic, lemon, and local herbs.
- Taste: The souvlaki is flavorful and aromatic, with a smoky char from the grill and a tender, juicy texture.
- Where to Try: Many local souvlaki stands and grill houses offer this specialty, often served with pita bread and fresh vegetables.

7. Local Wines and Spirits
- Description: Skopelos is known for its local wines and spirits, including the aromatic white wine and the traditional Greek spirit, ouzo.
- Ingredients: Local grapes for wine, and a blend of herbs and spices for ouzo.

- Taste: The wines are typically crisp and refreshing, while the ouzo has a distinct anise flavor, perfect for sipping.
- Where to Try: Enjoy local wines and ouzo at tavernas, bars, and restaurants, or visit local wineries for a taste of Skopelos's wine culture.

8. Honey and Nut Pastries (Sweets)
- Description: Traditional Greek sweets often feature honey, nuts, and sometimes pastry, providing a sweet and rich end to a meal.
- Ingredients: Honey, walnuts, almonds, filo dough, and various spices.
- Taste: Sweet and sticky with a rich, nutty flavor, these pastries are often enjoyed with a cup of coffee or as a dessert.
- Where to Try: Many bakeries and dessert shops in Skopelos offer a variety of these sweet treats, made with local honey and nuts.

9. Fresh Fish and Seafood
- Description: Skopelos's coastal location means that fresh fish and seafood are a highlight of the local cuisine, often prepared simply to showcase their natural flavors.
- Ingredients: Various types of fresh fish and seafood, including sea bream, calamari, and shrimp.

- Taste: The dishes are often lightly seasoned and grilled or fried, offering a taste of the sea that is fresh and delicious.
- Where to Try: Seafood restaurants and waterfront tavernas offer a range of fresh fish and seafood dishes, often served with a view of the Aegean Sea.

10. Local Olive Oil
- Description: Olive oil is a cornerstone of Greek cuisine, and Skopelos produces high-quality, flavorful olive oil that enhances many dishes.
- Ingredients: Extra virgin olive oil, often used as a dressing or cooking ingredient.
- Taste: Rich and fruity with a smooth, slightly peppery finish.
- Where to Try: Many restaurants use local olive oil, and it's also available for purchase at local markets and specialty shops.

Tips for Enjoying Traditional Skopelos Cuisine
- Try Local Taverns: For the most authentic experience, dine at family-run tavernas where traditional recipes and local ingredients are used.
- Ask for Recommendations: Don't hesitate to ask locals for their favorite dishes or eateries; they can provide great insights into the best culinary experiences.

- Pair with Local Wine: Enhance your meal by pairing traditional dishes with local Skopelos wines, which complement the flavors beautifully.

Savoring the traditional dishes of Skopelos is a culinary adventure that highlights the island's rich food heritage and local ingredients. From savory pies to fresh seafood, each dish offers a unique taste of Greek culture and hospitality.

Best Local Taverns, Cafes, and Fine Dining Spots

Skopelos offers a diverse range of dining options that cater to all tastes and budgets. Whether you're looking for a traditional tavern, a cozy café, or an upscale fine dining experience, the island's culinary scene has something to offer.

Local Taverns
1. Taverna To Helleniko
 - Overview: A beloved local tavern in Skopelos Town, known for its traditional Greek dishes and warm, welcoming atmosphere.
 - Specialties: Skopelitiki cheese pie, grilled octopus, and lamb with artichokes.
 - Highlights: Enjoy authentic Greek flavors in a charming setting, with friendly service and a menu that emphasizes local ingredients.

- Location: Skopelos Town, near the harbor.

2. Taverna Ouzeri Taverna
  - Overview: Situated in the heart of Skopelos Town, this taverna offers a classic Greek dining experience with a focus on fresh seafood.
  - Specialties: Fresh fish, calamari, and traditional Greek salads.
  - Highlights: Casual and relaxed atmosphere, with outdoor seating that allows you to enjoy the vibrant town ambiance.
  - Location: Skopelos Town, close to the main square.

3. Taverna Vrahos
  - Overview: Located by the beach in Agnondas, Vrahos is a great spot for enjoying a meal with a sea view.
  - Specialties: Grilled fish, stuffed zucchini flowers, and traditional meze plates.
  - Highlights: Beautiful seaside location, perfect for a sunset dinner, with a focus on fresh, local seafood.
  - Location: Agnondas Beach.

4. Taverna Kavouras
  - Overview: A rustic taverna located in the countryside, offering hearty traditional dishes in a homely setting.

- Specialties: Lamb dishes, home-cooked stews, and Greek mezze.
- Highlights: Cozy atmosphere with a focus on home-cooked meals and local flavors.
- Location: Near the village of Glossa.

Cafes

1. Cafe Kavouras
   - Overview: A charming café in Skopelos Town known for its relaxing ambiance and excellent coffee.
   - Specialties: Greek coffee, fresh pastries, and light bites.
   - Highlights: Perfect for a leisurely breakfast or afternoon coffee, with a lovely outdoor seating area.
   - Location: Skopelos Town, near the waterfront.

2. Cafe Sclavos
   - Overview: A popular spot for locals and visitors alike, offering a variety of coffee drinks and light meals.
   - Specialties: Espresso drinks, Greek sweets, and light sandwiches.
   - Highlights: Cozy interior with a friendly vibe, ideal for a casual coffee break or a snack.
   - Location: Skopelos Town, close to the main shopping area.

3. Cafe Mamma Mia

- Overview: This café is a great spot for enjoying a coffee or light meal in a relaxed setting.
- Specialties: Italian-style coffee, fresh pastries, and light salads.
- Highlights: A pleasant café with a relaxed atmosphere, perfect for a morning coffee or a light lunch.
- Location: Skopelos Town, near the marina.

4. Cafe Elies
- Overview: Nestled in a quiet area, Elies offers a tranquil setting with beautiful views and a focus on quality coffee.
- Specialties: Artisan coffee, homemade cakes, and light meals.
- Highlights: Scenic location and a great place for a peaceful coffee break away from the busier parts of town.
- Location: Skopelos Town, a short walk from the main square.

Fine Dining Spots
1. Restaurant Tzivaeri
- Overview: An elegant dining spot in Skopelos Town that combines fine dining with traditional Greek cuisine.
- Specialties: Gourmet versions of classic Greek dishes, such as slow-cooked lamb and seafood pasta.

- Highlights: Stylish setting with a focus on presentation and quality ingredients, offering an upscale dining experience.
- Location: Skopelos Town, near the main harbor.

2. Restaurant Panorama
- Overview: Located on a hillside with stunning views, Panorama offers a refined dining experience with a focus on fresh, local ingredients.
- Specialties: Grilled seafood, gourmet salads, and traditional Greek dishes with a modern twist.
- Highlights: Breathtaking views of the island and the sea, combined with an elegant and comfortable dining environment.
- Location: Skopelos Town, on a hill overlooking the bay.

3. Restaurant Asterias
- Overview: Situated on the beach in Panormos, Asterias provides a sophisticated dining experience with a focus on seafood and local produce.
- Specialties: Fresh seafood platters, grilled fish, and creative appetizers.
- Highlights: Beautiful beachfront location with an upscale menu and an elegant atmosphere.
- Location: Panormos Beach.

4. Restaurant Agnondas

- Overview: A fine dining establishment located in Agnondas, offering a menu that blends traditional Greek flavors with contemporary techniques.
- Specialties: Seafood risotto, lamb with herbs, and inventive starters.
- Highlights: Refined dining experience with a focus on high-quality ingredients and innovative presentations.
- Location: Agnondas Beach area.

Booking Tips
- Reservations: For fine dining spots, it's advisable to make reservations in advance, especially during peak tourist seasons.
- Local Recommendations: Ask locals for their favorite dining spots; they can offer great insights and hidden gems.
- Special Dietary Needs: If you have dietary restrictions, check with the restaurant in advance to ensure they can accommodate your needs.

Local Experiences
- Traditional Meze: When dining at tavernas, try a selection of meze (small dishes) to experience a variety of local flavors.
- Fresh Seafood: Enjoy fresh seafood dishes, particularly in coastal areas, where you can taste the catch of the day.

- Local Wine: Pair your meals with local wines to enhance your dining experience and savor the unique flavors of Skopelos.

Exploring the diverse dining options in Skopelos allows you to experience the island's rich culinary traditions and enjoy a range of flavors, from traditional Greek dishes to sophisticated fine dining. Whether you're seeking a casual café, a charming taverna, or an upscale restaurant, Skopelos has something to satisfy every palate.

Fresh Seafood And Farm-to-Table Restaurants

Skopelos, with its picturesque coastline and lush countryside, offers an exceptional culinary experience centered around fresh seafood and farm-to-table dining. The island's restaurants highlight the bounty of the Aegean Sea and the richness of local produce, providing a true taste of Greek gastronomy.

Fresh Seafood Restaurants
1. Taverna Ouzeri Taverna
 - Overview: Located in the heart of Skopelos Town, Ouzeri Taverna specializes in fresh seafood caught daily from the Aegean Sea.
 - Specialties: Grilled octopus, sea bream, calamari, and shrimp.
 - Highlights: The restaurant's open-air seating offers views of the bustling town, making it a great spot to enjoy a seafood feast while soaking in the local ambiance.
 - Location: Skopelos Town, close to the main square.

2. Taverna Vrahos
 - Overview: Situated in Agnondas Beach, Vrahos offers a picturesque seaside setting with a focus on freshly caught seafood.
 - Specialties: Grilled fish, stuffed calamari, and seafood pasta.
 - Highlights: Enjoy your meal with a view of the tranquil beach and the Aegean Sea, complemented by a relaxed, friendly atmosphere.
 - Location: Agnondas Beach.

3. Restaurant Asterias
  - Overview: Located on Panormos Beach, Asterias provides a sophisticated dining experience centered around the freshest seafood available.
  - Specialties: Seafood platters, grilled octopus, and seafood risotto.
  - Highlights: Elegant beachfront setting, ideal for a refined seafood dining experience with stunning sea views.
  - Location: Panormos Beach.

4. Taverna Agnondas
  - Overview: Found in Agnondas, this taverna focuses on delivering fresh seafood dishes with a touch of modern culinary flair.
  - Specialties: Grilled sea bass, seafood stew, and shrimp saganaki.
  - Highlights: A well-regarded spot for its high-quality seafood and innovative dishes, set in a charming seaside location.
  - Location: Agnondas Beach area.

5. Taverna To Kastro
  - Overview: A family-run taverna in Skopelos Town known for its fresh seafood and traditional Greek recipes.
  - Specialties: Fresh fish of the day, calamari, and seafood meze.

- Highlights: Authentic Greek atmosphere with a focus on fresh, locally sourced seafood and friendly service.

- Location: Skopelos Town, near the harbor.

Farm-to-Table Restaurants

1. Restaurant Tzivaeri

- Overview: Tzivaeri, located in Skopelos Town, emphasizes farm-to-table dining with a menu crafted from local produce and traditional Greek recipes.

- Specialties: Slow-cooked lamb, vegetable moussaka, and seasonal Greek salads.

- Highlights: The restaurant showcases the best of local produce and traditional flavors, with an elegant and comfortable dining environment.

- Location: Skopelos Town, near the waterfront.

2. Taverna Kavouras

- Overview: Nestled in the countryside near Glossa, Kavouras offers a rustic farm-to-table dining experience featuring homegrown ingredients and traditional recipes.

- Specialties: Roasted lamb, homemade pies, and fresh vegetables.

- Highlights: The taverna's focus on locally sourced ingredients and home-cooked meals provides a genuine taste of Greek rural cuisine.

- Location: Near Glossa Village.

3. Restaurant Elies
   - Overview: Elies, located in Skopelos Town, combines modern dining with a farm-to-table approach, offering dishes made from locally sourced ingredients.
   - Specialties: Farm-fresh salads, grilled meats, and seasonal vegetables.
   - Highlights: A modern and stylish setting that emphasizes the freshness and quality of local produce.
   - Location: Skopelos Town, a short walk from the main square.

4. Taverna To Helleniko
   - Overview: Situated in Skopelos Town, To Helleniko is known for its commitment to using fresh, local ingredients in traditional Greek dishes.
   - Specialties: Skopelitiki cheese pie, grilled meats, and fresh salads.
   - Highlights: Traditional Greek dishes prepared with locally sourced ingredients, offering an authentic taste of Skopelos.
   - Location: Skopelos Town, near the harbor.

5. Taverna Vasilis
   - Overview: Located in the countryside, Vasilis offers a true farm-to-table experience with a focus

on seasonal ingredients and traditional Greek cooking.
- Specialties: Hearty stews, fresh salads, and grilled meats.
- Highlights: The taverna's emphasis on farm-fresh ingredients and traditional recipes makes it a great spot for a rustic dining experience.
- Location: Rural area near Skopelos Town.

Tips for Enjoying Fresh Seafood and Farm-to-Table Dining
- Seasonal Availability: Fresh seafood and farm-to-table dishes are often seasonal, so be sure to ask about the day's specials and local ingredients.
- Local Recommendations: Don't hesitate to ask locals for their favorite spots or specialties; they can provide valuable insights and help you discover hidden gems.
- Pair with Local Wine: Enhance your dining experience by pairing your meal with local Skopelos wines, which complement both seafood and farm-to-table dishes beautifully.

Local Experiences
- Seafood Markets: Visit local seafood markets to see the day's catch and learn more about the local fishing practices.
- Farm Visits: Some farm-to-table restaurants may offer tours or visits to local farms, providing a

deeper understanding of where your food comes from.

Exploring Skopelos's fresh seafood and farm-to-table restaurants offers a delightful culinary experience that highlights the island's rich natural resources and traditional flavors. Whether you're enjoying a seafood feast by the beach or savoring farm-fresh dishes in a cozy taverna, Skopelos provides a memorable dining experience that showcases the best of Greek cuisine.

Food Markets And Where To Find Local Ingredients

Skopelos is not only renowned for its picturesque landscapes and charming villages but also for its vibrant food markets that offer a taste of local life and a bounty of fresh ingredients. These markets are the perfect places to explore if you want to savor the authentic flavors of Skopelos.

1. Skopelos Town Market
- Overview: The heart of Skopelos's food scene, the Skopelos Town Market is where you'll find a variety of local produce, fresh seafood, and traditional Greek ingredients.
- What to Find:

- Fresh Seafood: Local fish, octopus, calamari, and shellfish.
 - Local Produce: Fresh fruits, vegetables, herbs, and greens from nearby farms.
 - Cheese and Dairy: Skopelos cheese, including the famous Skopelitiki cheese, and other dairy products.
 - Olive Oil and Spices: High-quality olive oil and an array of Greek spices and herbs.
- Location: Central Skopelos Town, near the main square and harbor.

2. Glossa Market
- Overview: Located in the village of Glossa, this market offers a more local, traditional experience with a focus on village-produced goods.
- What to Find:
 - Homemade Preserves: Local jams, honey, and pickles made from regional fruits and vegetables.
 - Local Produce: Seasonal vegetables, fruits, and herbs grown in the surrounding countryside.
 - Bakery Items: Freshly baked bread and traditional Greek pastries.
- Location: Glossa Village, in the central market area.

3. Agnondas Market

- Overview: A smaller market near the coastal village of Agnondas, known for its seafood and local products.
- What to Find:
  - Seafood: Freshly caught fish and shellfish from local waters.
  - Local Ingredients: Olive oil, olives, and herbs.
  - Local Specialties: Regional snacks and homemade products from local vendors.
- Location: Agnondas Beach area, near the harbor.

4. Traditional Greek Food Stores
- Overview: Scattered throughout Skopelos, these stores specialize in traditional Greek ingredients and are great for finding authentic products.
- What to Find:
  - Greek Olive Oil: Premium extra virgin olive oil produced on the island.
  - Greek Spices and Herbs: Oregano, thyme, and other herbs used in traditional Greek cooking.
  - Local Wine: Wines produced on Skopelos and the surrounding islands.
  - Traditional Products: Items like feta cheese, yogurt, and local pastries.
- Locations: Various locations throughout Skopelos Town and other villages.

5. Farm Stands and Local Producers

- Overview: Visit farm stands and local producers in the countryside for fresh, farm-to-table ingredients and specialty products.
- What to Find:
  - Fresh Vegetables and Fruits: Seasonal produce directly from local farms.
  - Homemade Products: Local cheeses, cured meats, and artisanal bread.
  - Herbs and Greens: Fresh herbs and leafy greens grown in the island's fertile soil.
- Locations: Countryside around Skopelos, particularly near Glossa and other rural areas.

6. Local Olive Oil Presses
- Overview: Skopelos is known for its high-quality olive oil, and visiting an olive oil press can provide insight into the production process and allow you to purchase fresh oil directly from the source.
- What to Find:
  - Extra Virgin Olive Oil: Freshly pressed, high-quality olive oil.
  - Olive Oil Products: Various products made from olive oil, such as soaps and skincare items.
- Locations: Olive oil presses are located in the countryside and may offer tours or tastings.

7. Tips for Shopping at Food Markets

- Ask for Recommendations: Local vendors are often happy to share their recommendations and provide information about their products.
- Bargain Wisely: While bargaining is not always expected, polite negotiation can sometimes lead to better deals.
- Try Before You Buy: Many markets and stores offer samples, so take advantage of this to ensure the quality of the products.

8. Exploring Local Ingredients
- Olives and Olive Oil: Skopelos is known for its excellent olive oil, a staple in Greek cuisine. Look for locally produced extra virgin olive oil and enjoy its rich flavor in your meals.
- Cheese: Skopelitiki cheese is a local specialty with a unique flavor that's a must-try. It's used in various dishes, including the famous cheese pie.
- Seafood: Fresh seafood is a highlight of Skopelos's cuisine. Try local fish and shellfish to experience the best of the Aegean Sea.
- Herbs and Spices: Greek cooking relies heavily on fresh herbs like oregano, thyme, and rosemary. These are widely available and add authentic flavor to dishes.

Exploring the food markets and local producers in Skopelos offers a fantastic opportunity to experience the island's culinary culture and discover fresh, high-quality ingredients. Whether you're shopping for seafood, local produce, or traditional Greek products, the markets provide a vibrant and authentic taste of Skopelos's food scene.

Chapter 6

ADVENTURES: SKOPELOS AT ITS WILDEST

Top Beaches: Sandy Spots And Secluded Coves

Skopelos is known for its pristine beaches, where turquoise waters meet lush green landscapes. Whether you're looking for expansive sandy shores or hidden coves, the island offers a wide variety of beach experiences, each perfect for an adventure-filled day.

1. Panormos Beach: Vibrant and Family-Friendly
- Overview: Panormos Beach is one of the most popular sandy beaches in Skopelos, perfect for

families and travelers looking for a lively yet relaxing day by the sea.

- Features:

  - Crystal-Clear Waters: Ideal for swimming and snorkeling, with calm waters that are safe for all ages.
  - Sunbeds and Amenities: Panormos offers sunbeds, umbrellas, and beach bars for convenience and relaxation.
  - Scenic Backdrop: Surrounded by lush hillsides, providing a beautiful green contrast to the clear blue sea.

- Adventure Activities:

  - Snorkeling: The clear waters make Panormos great for underwater exploration.
  - Kayaking: Available for rent, allowing you to explore nearby coves.

- Location: About 12 km from Skopelos Town, easily accessible by car or bus.

2. Stafilos Beach: Rugged Beauty with a Historical Twist

- Overview: Stafilos Beach is a stunning mix of sandy and pebbled shores, named after the legendary Minoan prince Stafilos, whose tomb is said to have been discovered here.
- Features:

- Golden Sands and Pebbles: A perfect combination for sunbathers and those who enjoy the rustic feel of a pebbled beach.
- Cultural Significance: Close to an ancient archaeological site, adding a historical element to your beach day.
- Cliffside Views: The beach is nestled beneath cliffs, providing breathtaking views as you descend to the shore.
- Adventure Activities:
  - Hiking: There are scenic trails leading from the beach to the nearby Velanio Beach.
  - Swimming: The waters are shallow near the shore, making it ideal for swimming.
- Location: 4 km from Skopelos Town, accessible by a short drive and a scenic walk down to the beach.

3. Kastani Beach: Famous from "Mamma Mia!"
- Overview: Known as the beach where scenes from the movie Mamma Mia were filmed, Kastani Beach is a picturesque sandy spot with clear waters and a touch of Hollywood magic.
- Features:
  - Fine Golden Sand: One of the few truly sandy beaches on the island, perfect for sunbathing and lounging.

- Beach Bar: Offers refreshments and snacks, enhancing your beach experience with a bit of luxury.
  - Shallow, Clear Waters: Ideal for swimming, with gently sloping sands underfoot.
- Adventure Activities:
  - Paddleboarding: Calm waters make this an ideal spot for trying out paddleboarding.
  - Scenic Walks: Stroll along the beach or hike up to nearby viewpoints for amazing coastal vistas.
- Location: Located about 15 km from Skopelos Town, easily reachable by car or bus.

4. Hovolo Beach: Secluded and Stunning
- Overview: Hovolo Beach is a hidden gem, tucked away behind towering white cliffs. Its remote location makes it one of the most secluded and peaceful beaches on Skopelos.
- Features:
  - Soft Sands and Crystal Waters: The soft sand and clear waters make it a paradise for beachgoers seeking tranquility.
  - Natural Beauty: The surrounding cliffs create a dramatic backdrop, perfect for photography and exploration.
  - Secluded Atmosphere: Due to its remote access, the beach is often less crowded, offering privacy and peace.
- Adventure Activities:

- Cliff Jumping: For the daring, there are spots along the cliffs where you can safely jump into the water.
- Exploring Caves: The beach has several small caves along the shoreline, perfect for curious adventurers.
- Location: Near Elios Village on the western side of the island, accessible by a short hike from the main road.

5. Milia Beach: The Longest Sandy Shore
- Overview: Milia Beach is one of the longest and most spacious beaches on Skopelos, offering plenty of room to spread out and enjoy a day of sun and sea.
- Features:
  - White Sands and Pebbles: A combination of soft sands and white pebbles, creating a beautiful shoreline.
  - Beach Bars and Sunbeds: Milia offers full amenities, including sunbeds and beach bars.
  - Scenic Views: The beach provides views of nearby Dassia islet and the surrounding forested hills.
- Adventure Activities:
  - Snorkeling: The clear waters around the islet of Dassia are perfect for snorkeling and exploring marine life.

- Beach Volleyball: With its spacious layout, Milia is a great spot for beach sports.
  - Location: Located about 14 km from Skopelos Town, accessible by car or bus.

6. Limnonari Beach: A Natural Lagoon
  - Overview: Limnonari Beach is known for its unique lagoon-like waters, surrounded by dense pine forests, creating a peaceful and naturally beautiful environment.
  - Features:
    - Soft Sands: The sandy shore is perfect for lounging and sunbathing.
    - Calm, Shallow Waters: Ideal for families and those looking for a relaxing swim.
    - Natural Beauty: The beach is framed by pine trees, offering both sun and shade.
  - Adventure Activities:
    - Kayaking: Explore the lagoon-like waters and nearby coves by kayak.
    - Hiking: Trails around the beach provide excellent hiking opportunities with scenic views.
  - Location: Located 9 km from Skopelos Town, accessible by car.

7. Velanio Beach: Skopelos's Only Official Nudist Beach
  - Overview: Velanio Beach is Skopelos's only official nudist beach, offering a serene and

uncrowded environment for those looking to connect with nature.
- Features:
  - Secluded and Peaceful: Located beyond Stafilos Beach, Velanio offers a secluded and quiet atmosphere.
  - Crystal Waters: The beach is famous for its clear, azure waters, ideal for swimming and snorkeling.
  - Natural Beauty: Surrounded by pine-covered cliffs, it offers a dramatic natural setting.
- Adventure Activities:
  - Snorkeling: The rocky seabed around the beach is perfect for snorkeling enthusiasts.
  - Wild Swimming: The calm and clean waters make Velanio an ideal spot for open water swimming.
- Location: Accessible by walking from Stafilos Beach, about 4.5 km from Skopelos Town.

8. Agnondas Beach: A Cozy Cove for Seafood Lovers
- Overview: Agnondas Beach is a small and quiet beach, famous for its waterfront tavernas where you can enjoy fresh seafood after a swim.
- Features:
  - Pebbled Shore: A mix of pebbles and sand, creating a cozy spot for lounging.

- Waterfront Dining: Several tavernas line the beach, offering fresh seafood and traditional Greek dishes.
- Calm Waters: Ideal for swimming and relaxing in the shallow, peaceful sea.
- Adventure Activities:
  - Fishing: This quiet cove is a great spot to try your hand at fishing.
  - Boat Trips: Take a boat trip from Agnondas to explore nearby coves and beaches.
- Location: Located 8 km from Skopelos Town, easily accessible by car or bus.

Tips for Beach Adventures in Skopelos
- Best Time to Visit: The best time to explore Skopelos's beaches is from May to September, when the weather is warm and the waters are calm.
- Bring Snorkeling Gear: Many of the beaches on Skopelos have clear waters perfect for snorkeling, so bring your own gear to explore the underwater world.
- Pack Essentials: For more secluded beaches like Hovolo and Velanio, bring your own water, snacks, and shade as facilities are limited.

Skopelos offers a diverse range of beach experiences, from vibrant sandy shores to hidden coves, making it a perfect destination for beach adventures. Whether you're seeking relaxation or exploration, the island's stunning beaches provide endless opportunities for enjoying the sun, sea, and natural beauty of this Aegean paradise.

Hiking Trails With Stunning Views

Skopelos is a paradise for hiking enthusiasts, offering a variety of trails that wind through its lush landscapes, dense pine forests, and olive groves, leading to breathtaking panoramic views of the Aegean Sea, charming villages, and ancient ruins. Whether you're a seasoned hiker or just looking for a leisurely walk, Skopelos's hiking trails provide a serene way to explore the island's natural beauty.

1. Mount Delphi Trail: The Highest Point on Skopelos
- Overview: For hikers seeking a challenge and unparalleled views, the Mount Delphi trail is the

perfect adventure. Standing at 681 meters, Mount Delphi is the highest peak on Skopelos, offering a panoramic view of the island and the surrounding sea.

- Trail Features:
  - Length: Approximately 4-5 hours round trip, depending on your pace and starting point.
  - Terrain: Moderate to challenging, with rocky paths and steep inclines as you approach the summit.
  - Highlights: From the peak, you can see the entire island, neighboring Alonissos, and even parts of the mainland on clear days.
  - Nature and Wildlife: As you ascend, you'll pass through olive groves and pine forests, home to native birds and wildlife.
  - Location: The trail starts near the village of Glossa, and signage will guide you toward the peak.

2. Skopelos Town to Stafilos Beach: A Coastal Walk with History
- Overview: This trail offers a more leisurely hike, taking you from Skopelos Town to Stafilos Beach along a scenic coastal path. It's an excellent option for combining history, culture, and natural beauty.
- Trail Features:
  - Length: Around 6 km one way, about 2 hours of walking.

- Terrain: Easy to moderate, with well-trodden paths and some uphill sections.
- Highlights: Along the way, you'll pass olive trees, small chapels, and ancient ruins. The hike ends at Stafilos Beach, where you can relax and swim in the crystal-clear waters.
- Historical Significance: Stafilos is named after the legendary Minoan prince Stafilos, whose tomb was discovered here.
- Location: The trail starts in Skopelos Town and leads south towards Stafilos Beach.

3. Glossa to Agios Ioannis Chapel: The Iconic "Mamma Mia!" Hike
- Overview: This trail takes you from the charming village of Glossa to the famous Agios Ioannis Chapel, perched on a rock overlooking the Aegean Sea. The chapel gained international fame as a filming location for the movie *Mamma Mia!*.
- Trail Features:
  - Length: Approximately 2.5 km, about 1.5 hours of walking.
  - Terrain: Moderate, with some steep sections, especially as you approach the chapel's 198 steps leading to its entrance.
  - Highlights: The breathtaking views from the top of the chapel are among the most iconic on the island, offering sweeping vistas of the sea and

neighboring islands. The hike also passes through lush landscapes, olive groves, and small vineyards.
 - Cultural Importance: Agios Ioannis is not only known for its cinematic fame but also for its serene and spiritual atmosphere.
 - Location: The trail begins in Glossa and ends at the chapel on the northeastern coast of Skopelos.

4. The Monasteries Trail: A Spiritual and Scenic Journey
 - Overview: This trail takes hikers through Skopelos's spiritual heart, connecting several of the island's most important monasteries. As you hike, you'll experience peaceful forest paths, stunning viewpoints, and centuries-old religious sites.
 - Trail Features:
   - Length: About 8 km round trip, approximately 3-4 hours of walking.
   - Terrain: Easy to moderate, with some inclines. The trail is well-marked and accessible to most hikers.
 - Highlights:
   - Evangelistria Monastery: A fortress-like structure with beautiful architecture and a tranquil atmosphere.
   - Monastery of Prodromos: Nestled in pine forests, offering quiet reflection and scenic surroundings.

- Panagia Livadiotissa Monastery: One of the oldest monasteries on the island, with sweeping views of the coast.
- Views: The trail offers stunning vistas of Skopelos Town and the Aegean Sea, making it a rewarding experience for hikers.
- Location: The trail starts just outside Skopelos Town, heading inland towards the monasteries.

5. The Coastal Path to Panormos Beach: A Tranquil Seaside Stroll
- Overview: For those seeking a more relaxed hike, the coastal path to Panormos Beach offers a peaceful walk along the seaside, passing through olive groves and pine forests. It's perfect for a leisurely afternoon adventure.
- Trail Features:
  - Length: Approximately 5 km, about 1.5 to 2 hours of walking.
  - Terrain: Easy, with mostly flat terrain and well-trodden paths.
  - Highlights: As you walk along the coast, you'll enjoy views of the sparkling Aegean Sea and Skopelos's lush hillsides. The hike ends at Panormos Beach, where you can relax on the sandy shore or enjoy a meal at one of the nearby tavernas.
  - Beach Adventure: Panormos Beach is known for its crystal-clear waters, making it an ideal spot for a post-hike swim or snorkeling session.

- Location: The trail starts near Elios village and follows the coast towards Panormos Beach.

6. Palouki Mountain Trail: A Hike to Ancient Ruins and Panoramic Views
- Overview: Palouki Mountain is one of Skopelos's lesser-known hiking spots, but it offers a rewarding experience for those who venture there. The hike takes you past ancient ruins, including old monasteries and chapels, and rewards you with panoramic views of the island.
- Trail Features:
  - Length: Around 10 km round trip, approximately 4-5 hours of walking.
  - Terrain: Moderate to challenging, with rocky paths and steep sections as you ascend the mountain.
  - Highlights: The hike takes you past the ruins of ancient monasteries and offers spectacular views of Skopelos Town, the harbor, and the surrounding islands. You'll also pass through olive groves, vineyards, and pine forests, giving you a true taste of Skopelos's natural beauty.
  - Cultural Significance: The ruins of old monasteries, such as Timios Prodromos and the Church of Agia Barbara, offer a glimpse into Skopelos's spiritual past.
- Location: The trail starts near Skopelos Town, leading east toward Palouki Mountain.

7. Agnondas to Limnonari Beach: A Coastal Adventure
- Overview: This coastal trail connects the small fishing village of Agnondas with the secluded Limnonari Beach. It's a great option for hikers who want to explore Skopelos's coastline and enjoy a swim in a calm, picturesque bay.
- Trail Features:
  - Length: About 3 km one way, roughly 1.5 hours of walking.
- Terrain: Easy to moderate, with some rocky paths along the coast.
- Highlights: The trail follows the coastline, offering stunning views of the Aegean Sea and the surrounding cliffs. The hike ends at Limnonari Beach, a tranquil bay with calm waters perfect for swimming and snorkeling.
- Relaxation: After your hike, enjoy a meal at one of the beachside tavernas, offering fresh seafood and local dishes.
- Location: The trail starts in Agnondas and follows the coast west to Limnonari Beach.

Tips for Hiking in Skopelos
- Best Time to Hike: The best months for hiking in Skopelos are from May to October, when the weather is warm but not too hot. Early mornings or

late afternoons are ideal for avoiding the midday heat.

- What to Bring: Comfortable hiking shoes, plenty of water, sunscreen, a hat, and a map or GPS. Many of the trails are well-marked, but it's always good to have a navigation tool just in case.

- Respect Nature: Stick to designated paths to avoid disturbing the island's delicate ecosystems. Take any trash with you, and avoid lighting fires during dry periods.

- Local Guides: If you prefer a guided experience, local hiking tours are available and can provide deeper insight into the history, culture, and nature of Skopelos.

Skopelos's hiking trails offer the perfect blend of natural beauty, cultural exploration, and adventure. From coastal walks to mountain climbs, these trails provide stunning views and a unique way to experience the island's diverse landscapes. Whether you're hiking to secluded beaches, ancient ruins, or scenic mountaintops, the adventures you'll find on Skopelos's trails are sure to leave lasting memories.

Water Sports: Kayaking, Snorkeling And Sailing

Skopelos, with its crystal-clear waters, hidden coves, and stunning coastal landscapes, is a haven for water sports enthusiasts. Whether you're paddling through the island's serene waters in a kayak, snorkeling in vibrant underwater ecosystems, or sailing along the picturesque coastline, Skopelos offers a range of water adventures for travelers seeking both relaxation and excitement.

Kayaking: Exploring Skopelos's Hidden Coves and Coastlines

Kayaking in Skopelos allows you to experience the island's coastline from a unique perspective. Paddling through calm, clear waters, you can access secluded beaches and coves that are otherwise unreachable by foot or road. It's an adventure perfect for beginners and seasoned kayakers alike.

1. Best Kayaking Spots in Skopelos
- Panormos Bay: Known for its calm waters and scenic surroundings, Panormos Bay is ideal for leisurely kayaking. Paddle along the coast and discover hidden coves and small, private beaches.
- Milia Beach to Kastani Beach: A popular kayaking route, this stretch allows you to explore the iconic Kastani Beach, made famous by the Mamma Mia! movie. The short paddle from Milia Beach to Kastani Beach offers stunning views of the coastline and crystal-clear waters.
- Stafilos to Velanio Beach: Paddle from the historical Stafilos Beach to the tranquil Velanio Beach, Skopelos's only official nudist beach. The trip offers peaceful surroundings and beautiful cliffs along the way.
- Hovolo Beach: For more adventurous kayakers, the trip to Hovolo Beach offers an unforgettable journey. This hidden gem is tucked away and difficult to reach by foot, making it a perfect destination for kayakers.

2. Kayaking Tours and Rentals
Several local companies offer kayak rentals and guided tours, ensuring a safe and informative experience:

- Kayak Skopelos: One of the most popular providers, offering both rentals and guided tours. You can choose from half-day or full-day trips, with options to explore caves, isolated beaches, and nearby islets.
- Glossa Kayak Tours: Departing from Glossa, these tours take you through northern Skopelos's lesser-known spots, giving you access to pristine coves and secret beaches.

3. What to Expect
- Duration: Kayaking trips range from a few hours to full-day excursions.
- Difficulty: Most kayaking routes are suitable for beginners, thanks to Skopelos's calm waters, but there are also more challenging routes for experienced paddlers.
- Best Time: The best time for kayaking is from May to September when the sea is calm and the weather is warm.

Snorkeling: Discover Skopelos's Vibrant Underwater Life

Snorkeling in Skopelos offers an intimate way to explore the island's underwater world, from colorful marine life to rocky reefs. With its pristine waters and abundant sea life, Skopelos is a snorkeling paradise for both beginners and experienced snorkelers.

1. Top Snorkeling Spots in Skopelos
- Agnondas Beach: Known for its calm waters and easy access, Agnondas Beach is a great spot for beginner snorkelers. The underwater rock formations and clear waters make it an ideal location for spotting fish and marine life.
- Stafilos Beach: The rocky seabed near Stafilos Beach provides excellent conditions for snorkeling. You can explore the area's caves and small reefs while observing a variety of fish and underwater creatures.
- Velanio Beach: Velanio Beach offers some of the clearest waters on the island, making it a top snorkeling destination. The secluded nature of the beach means fewer crowds and undisturbed underwater ecosystems.
- Panormos Bay: Known for its turquoise waters, Panormos Bay is a popular snorkeling destination. The rocks near the shoreline create natural hiding places for fish, and the bay's calm waters allow for easy exploration.
- Limnonari Beach: With its lagoon-like waters, Limnonari Beach is perfect for snorkeling. The sandy seabed is home to a variety of small fish and marine plants, making it an exciting spot for underwater exploration.

2. What to Expect

- Marine Life: Expect to see a variety of fish species, including sea bream, groupers, and occasionally octopuses. The rocky sea floor around Skopelos's beaches also provides habitats for crabs and other sea creatures.
- Gear: Most of Skopelos's beaches have nearby shops or rental facilities offering snorkeling gear, but you can also bring your own for more flexibility.
- Visibility: The waters around Skopelos are known for their clarity, with visibility often reaching 20 meters or more, especially in the summer months.
- Best Time: The best time for snorkeling is during the summer months, from June to September, when the water is warm and visibility is at its peak.

Sailing: Embrace the Freedom of the Aegean Sea
Sailing around Skopelos provides the ultimate adventure for exploring the island's coastline and nearby islands. With its deep-blue waters, secluded bays, and proximity to other beautiful islands in the Northern Sporades archipelago, Skopelos is a sailor's dream.

1. Sailing Routes and Destinations
- Skopelos to Alonissos: A popular sailing route takes you from Skopelos to the nearby island of Alonissos, known for its Marine Park and unspoiled natural beauty. The journey offers a mix of stunning

views, swimming stops, and the chance to spot dolphins.
- Around Skopelos Island: A full-day sail around Skopelos offers you the chance to explore hidden beaches, sea caves, and isolated coves that are only accessible by boat. Some of the highlights include the beaches of Hovolo, Perivoliou, and the rocky cliffs of Glossa.
- Skopelos to Skiathos: Another exciting sailing route is from Skopelos to the bustling island of Skiathos. Along the way, you'll pass secluded beaches and scenic coastlines, with plenty of opportunities for swimming and snorkeling.
- Mamma Mia! Sailing Route: For fans of the Mamma Mia! movie, several sailing tours take you to the filming locations, including the famous Kastani Beach and the Agios Ioannis Chapel, perched on a cliff overlooking the sea.

2. Sailing Tours and Rentals
- Skopelos Sailing: Offering private and shared sailing tours around the island and to nearby destinations like Alonissos and Skiathos. You can enjoy a day of sailing, swimming, and exploring hidden spots along the coast.
- Charter a Yacht: For those with sailing experience, chartering a yacht gives you complete freedom to explore the Northern Sporades at your own pace.

Several companies in Skopelos offer yacht rentals, with options for bareboat or crewed charters.
- Day Cruises: If you're new to sailing or prefer a guided experience, day cruises are available from Skopelos Town and Glossa. These cruises often include stops at secluded beaches, lunch on board, and plenty of time for swimming and snorkeling.

3. What to Expect
- Duration: Sailing trips range from half-day excursions to multi-day journeys around the Sporades islands.
- Sailing Conditions: The Aegean Sea around Skopelos is generally calm during the summer, with light winds that are perfect for sailing. However, sailors should be prepared for occasional strong winds, especially in late summer.
- Wildlife Spotting: Keep an eye out for dolphins, sea turtles, and seabirds while sailing. The waters around Skopelos and Alonissos are part of a protected marine area, home to diverse marine life.

Tips for Water Sports in Skopelos
- Best Time to Visit: The ideal months for water sports in Skopelos are from May to September, when the sea is warm, and the weather is pleasant.
- Safety First: Always wear life jackets when kayaking or sailing, and be mindful of weather conditions. When snorkeling, avoid touching

marine life or coral, as these ecosystems are delicate.

- Guided Tours: For beginners or those unfamiliar with the area, guided tours are highly recommended for kayaking, snorkeling, and sailing, ensuring safety and the best experiences.

Skopelos's stunning coastline and crystal-clear waters make it the perfect destination for water sports adventures. Whether you're paddling along secluded beaches in a kayak, snorkeling in vibrant underwater worlds, or sailing around the island's scenic shores, Skopelos offers unforgettable experiences for water lovers of all skill levels. With its mix of calm seas, hidden coves, and rich marine life, the island is a water sports paradise waiting to be explored.

Day Trips And Boat Excursions To Neighboring Islands

Skopelos, nestled in the Northern Sporades archipelago, is not just a destination for exploring its own natural beauty but also serves as a gateway to nearby islands. Day trips and boat excursions to the surrounding islands-like Skiathos, Alonissos, and smaller, more remote islets-provide travelers with the opportunity to experience more of the region's diverse landscapes, wildlife, and cultural heritage. Whether you're looking to relax on a quiet beach, explore marine parks, or visit charming villages, Skopelos offers easy access to a variety of nearby islands.

Skiathos: Bustling Beaches and Vibrant Nightlife
Skiathos, just a short ferry ride from Skopelos, is the most cosmopolitan of the Northern Sporades islands. Known for its vibrant atmosphere, golden beaches, and lively nightlife, Skiathos makes for an exciting day trip filled with activities and beautiful scenery.

1. Highlights of Skiathos
- Koukounaries Beach: One of Greece's most famous beaches, Koukounaries is a long stretch of fine golden sand backed by a pine forest. It's a must-visit for beach lovers, offering plenty of water sports, beach bars, and sunbeds.
- Skiathos Town: Explore the charming streets of Skiathos Town, filled with shops, cafes, and traditional tavernas. Visit the Bourtzi Peninsula, a picturesque site with ruins of a Venetian fortress and a scenic view of the harbor.
- Lalaria Beach: Accessible only by boat, this stunning beach is famous for its dramatic white cliffs, smooth pebbles, and crystal-clear waters. A visit to Lalaria Beach is a highlight of any Skiathos excursion.

- Monastery of Evangelistria: This 18th-century monastery is a peaceful retreat in the hills of Skiathos. It's known for its beautiful architecture and historical significance, including its role in the Greek War of Independence.

2. Getting to Skiathos
- Ferries and Boat Tours: Ferries run regularly between Skopelos and Skiathos, making it easy to organize a day trip. You can also book guided boat tours that include stops at Skiathos's top beaches and landmarks.
- Duration: The ferry ride takes around 30-45 minutes, making Skiathos an ideal destination for a full-day excursion from Skopelos.

Alonissos: Pristine Nature and Marine Life
Alonissos, located just to the east of Skopelos, is known for its unspoiled natural beauty and rich marine life. The island is home to the largest marine park in Europe, the National Marine Park of Alonissos and Northern Sporades, where visitors can explore protected waters and learn about the endangered Mediterranean monk seals. Alonissos is perfect for nature lovers, snorkelers, and those seeking a peaceful retreat.

1. Highlights of Alonissos

- National Marine Park of Alonissos: This marine park is a haven for biodiversity, offering visitors the chance to spot dolphins, rare bird species, and the elusive Mediterranean monk seal. Boat excursions to the park often include snorkeling or diving stops in the crystal-clear waters.
- Patitiri Town: The charming capital of Alonissos, Patitiri, is a picturesque harbor town with waterfront cafes and traditional houses. It's a great place to enjoy a leisurely lunch before exploring more of the island.
- Chora (Old Alonissos): Perched on a hilltop, Chora is the ancient village of Alonissos, offering stunning panoramic views of the sea. Wander through its narrow streets, lined with whitewashed houses, and enjoy the tranquility and beauty of this historical settlement.
- Secluded Beaches: Alonissos is known for its secluded beaches, such as Agios Dimitrios, Megalos Mourtias, and Leftos Gialos. These beaches offer a peaceful retreat, ideal for sunbathing, swimming, and snorkeling.

2. Boat Excursions to Alonissos
- Guided Tours: Many boat tours from Skopelos include stops at Alonissos, often combined with trips to the marine park or nearby islets. These tours typically depart from Skopelos Town or Glossa and include swimming, snorkeling, and lunch on board.

- Ferry Services: Ferries between Skopelos and Alonissos run several times a day, making it easy to plan a day trip to explore the island at your own pace.

Kyra Panagia Island: Untouched Paradise in the Marine Park

Kyra Panagia, also known as Pelagos, is a small, uninhabited island located within the National Marine Park of Alonissos and Northern Sporades. It's an untouched paradise, offering a glimpse into Greece's wilder side, with pristine beaches, a peaceful monastery, and clear waters ideal for swimming and snorkeling.

1. Highlights of Kyra Panagia
- Monastery of Kyra Panagia: This centuries-old monastery sits on a hill overlooking the sea. Although uninhabited, the monastery is well-maintained and open to visitors, offering a serene and spiritual atmosphere.
- Secluded Bays: The island is known for its secluded bays, perfect for a peaceful swim or simply relaxing on the beach. Agios Petros and Planitis Bay are two of the island's most beautiful spots, offering crystal-clear waters and scenic views.
- Snorkeling and Diving: The waters around Kyra Panagia are teeming with marine life, making it a

popular destination for snorkeling and diving. The area's underwater caves and rocky reefs offer excellent conditions for exploration.

2. Boat Excursions to Kyra Panagia
- Day Tours from Skopelos: Several boat tours offer trips to Kyra Panagia, often combined with visits to Alonissos and other nearby islets. These tours typically include stops for swimming, snorkeling, and exploring the island's natural beauty.
- Duration: As part of a day trip, you can expect to spend a few hours on Kyra Panagia, with ample time to explore its bays and the monastery.

Peristera Island: A Diver's Dream
Peristera is another small island located within the Alonissos Marine Park, known for its underwater archaeological sites and rich marine life. It's a must-visit destination for divers and snorkelers who want to explore ancient shipwrecks and submerged ruins.

1. Highlights of Peristera
- Peristera Shipwreck: One of the most famous underwater attractions in the area is the ancient shipwreck of Peristera. Dating back to the 5th century BC, this wreck is one of the largest and best-preserved ancient shipwrecks in the Aegean

Sea. Divers and snorkelers can explore the site, which is teeming with marine life.
- Secluded Beaches: Peristera also offers several secluded beaches, ideal for a quiet day of swimming and relaxation. The island's remote location means it's rarely crowded, providing a peaceful escape.
- Wildlife Spotting: The island is part of the marine park, so it's common to spot dolphins, sea turtles, and rare seabirds while sailing around Peristera.

2. Boat Excursions to Peristera
- Diving Tours: For those interested in exploring the Peristera shipwreck, several diving tours depart from Skopelos and Alonissos. These tours include all the necessary equipment and expert guides to ensure a safe and informative dive.
- Snorkeling and Swimming: If diving isn't your thing, you can still enjoy the waters around Peristera with a snorkeling or swimming excursion. Many boat tours include stops at the island's beaches and coves for a relaxing swim in the clear waters.

Skantzoura Island: A Remote Escape
Skantzoura, another uninhabited island in the Northern Sporades, is known for its rugged beauty and remote location. It's a popular destination for those seeking an off-the-beaten-path adventure,

with its rocky coastline, hidden coves, and rich marine biodiversity.

1. Highlights of Skantzoura
- Pristine Beaches: Skantzoura's beaches are some of the most secluded in the Sporades, offering visitors the chance to relax in complete tranquility. The island's rocky coastline also makes for excellent snorkeling opportunities.
- Monastery Ruins: The island is home to the ruins of an old monastery, adding a touch of history to your day trip. The remote and serene atmosphere makes it a peaceful place to explore.
- Birdwatching: Skantzoura is a haven for birdwatchers, with many rare species nesting on the island. The island's isolation has allowed its wildlife to thrive, making it a great spot for nature lovers.

2. Boat Excursions to Skantzoura
- Private Boat Tours: Skantzoura is often included in private boat tours of the Sporades, offering a more customized and intimate experience. These tours typically include stops for swimming, snorkeling, and exploring the island's untouched landscapes.
- Sailing Excursions: If you're looking for a more relaxed adventure, sailing tours often include a stop

at Skantzoura, allowing you to take in the island's beauty while enjoying the comforts of a sailboat.

Tips for Day Trips and Boat Excursions
- Booking in Advance: During the peak summer months (June to September), it's recommended to book boat tours and ferries in advance, as they can fill up quickly.
- Bring Essentials: For day trips, pack essentials like sunscreen, water, and a hat. Many of the islands have limited facilities, so it's best to be prepared.
- Snorkeling Gear: If you're planning to snorkel, consider bringing your own gear, though many tours provide equipment.

Skopelos's proximity to other stunning islands makes it the perfect base for island hopping in the Northern Sporades. Whether you're drawn to the lively atmosphere of Skiathos, the natural beauty of Alonissos, or the untouched wilderness of Kyra Panagia, day trips and boat excursions offer a wealth of adventures to explore. From relaxing on secluded beaches to discovering ancient shipwrecks, the islands surrounding Skopelos promise unforgettable experiences for every type of traveler.

Chapter 7

STAYING SAFE AND GREEN

Health And Safety Tips For Travelers

Skopelos is generally a safe destination, with low crime rates and a welcoming atmosphere. However, like any travel destination, it's important to take precautions to ensure your trip is safe and enjoyable. Below are essential health and safety tips for travelers visiting Skopelos.

1. Medical Care and Health Precautions
- Healthcare Facilities: Skopelos has basic healthcare facilities, including a small medical center in Skopelos Town and pharmacies scattered around the island. For more serious medical issues, you may need to travel to nearby islands like Skiathos or the mainland.

- Travel Insurance: It's recommended to have travel insurance that covers medical expenses. Ensure your insurance includes coverage for activities like hiking, swimming, or water sports.
- Pharmacies: Pharmacies are well-stocked with common medicines, but it's a good idea to bring any prescription medications you require. Always carry extra doses in case of delays or emergencies.
- Water Quality: Tap water in Skopelos is generally safe to drink, but bottled water is widely available and preferred by many locals and tourists, especially in remote areas.

2. Staying Safe Outdoors
- Sun Protection: Skopelos enjoys hot, sunny summers, so it's important to protect yourself from sunburn and heatstroke. Always wear sunscreen, sunglasses, and a hat when spending time outdoors, especially on the beach or while hiking. Seek shade during the hottest parts of the day (between 12 PM and 3 PM).
- Hydration: Stay hydrated, particularly if you are hiking or exploring under the sun. Carry a water bottle with you, and drink water regularly to prevent dehydration.
- Insects: Mosquitoes can be present, particularly in the evenings and near water. Pack insect repellent to avoid bites, and consider using mosquito nets or

sprays in your accommodation if you're staying in rural areas.
- Wildlife Awareness: Skopelos's natural landscapes are home to various wildlife, including snakes and lizards, especially in the countryside. While encounters with dangerous animals are rare, it's best to stay on marked trails when hiking and avoid tall grass or rocky areas where snakes may hide.

3. Road Safety and Transportation
- Car Rentals: If you're renting a car to explore Skopelos, be cautious on the island's narrow and winding roads, especially in mountainous areas. Drive slowly, as roads may be steep or lack guardrails. Ensure that your rental car is equipped with the necessary safety features, including seatbelts and functional brakes.
- Motorbikes and Scooters: Scooters are a popular way to get around the island, but always wear a helmet and drive carefully. The roads can be tricky, particularly if you're unfamiliar with local driving conditions.
- Public Transport: Buses on Skopelos are safe, reliable, and cost-effective. However, during peak tourist seasons, they may get crowded. Plan your trips to avoid the busiest times of day if possible.
- Walking at Night: Skopelos is very safe for walking at night, especially in well-lit areas like

Skopelos Town. However, if you're in more rural areas or walking along narrow roads, carry a flashlight and wear reflective clothing to stay visible.

4. Beach and Water Safety
- Swimming Precautions: While the beaches of Skopelos are generally safe, always be cautious when swimming, especially at beaches without lifeguards. Pay attention to any warning flags or signs about swimming conditions. If you're not a strong swimmer, avoid swimming in deep or rough waters.
- Water Sports: For those engaging in water sports such as kayaking, snorkeling, or paddleboarding, ensure you're using quality equipment and following safety instructions. It's advisable to book activities with certified tour operators.
- Jellyfish and Sea Urchins: Occasionally, jellyfish or sea urchins may be found in the waters around Skopelos. If stung, rinse the affected area with seawater (not freshwater) and seek medical advice if the sting causes severe pain or an allergic reaction. Wearing water shoes can help prevent stepping on sea urchins.
- Boat Safety: If you're renting a boat or going on a boat tour, follow all safety protocols, including wearing life jackets. The seas around Skopelos can

sometimes become choppy, so be mindful of weather conditions before heading out on the water.

5. Personal Safety and Crime Prevention
- Low Crime Rates: Skopelos is known for its low crime rate, and violent crime is extremely rare. Petty theft, such as pickpocketing, is also uncommon, but it's always wise to remain vigilant, especially in busy tourist areas.
- Protect Your Belongings: Keep your valuables, such as wallets, phones, and passports, secure when you're out exploring. Use hotel safes when available, and avoid carrying large sums of cash.
- Emergency Numbers: The emergency number for police, fire, and medical assistance in Greece is 112. Familiarize yourself with this number in case of any urgent situations.
- Traveling Solo: Skopelos is generally very safe for solo travelers, including women. Just follow common-sense precautions like avoiding isolated areas late at night and letting someone know your itinerary if you're going on hikes or boat trips alone.

6. Respecting Nature and the Environment
- Litter-Free Beaches: Skopelos's beaches and natural areas are pristine, and it's important to keep them that way. Always dispose of your trash properly, and avoid leaving waste behind, especially plastic.

- Forest Fire Prevention: In the dry summer months, the risk of forest fires is higher. Avoid starting fires in outdoor areas, and never throw cigarette butts or glass bottles in nature, as they can ignite dry vegetation.
- Preserving Marine Life: When snorkeling or diving, avoid touching or disturbing marine life, including corals and sea creatures. Skopelos is part of a marine park, so it's essential to respect the local ecosystem.

By following these health and safety tips, travelers can enjoy a worry-free experience in Skopelos while exploring its beaches, hiking trails, and villages. Staying prepared and cautious will ensure your trip is both enjoyable and safe.

Protecting The Environment: Eco-friendly Travel

Skopelos, known for its lush forests, crystal-clear waters, and pristine beaches, is a paradise for nature lovers. To preserve the island's natural beauty for future generations, eco-friendly travel practices are essential. By making conscious decisions about how you explore and interact with the environment, you can minimize your impact while enjoying everything Skopelos has to offer.

Sustainable Accommodation Choices

Choosing environmentally friendly accommodations is one of the most impactful ways to reduce your carbon footprint while traveling. Skopelos offers a variety of sustainable lodging options, from eco-friendly hotels to charming guesthouses committed to green practices.

1. Eco-Lodges and Sustainable Villas
- Eco-Lodges: Many eco-lodges on the island use renewable energy sources, such as solar panels, to power their facilities. These accommodations often integrate sustainable building materials and practices to blend harmoniously with the natural surroundings.
- Sustainable Villas: Some private villas are designed with sustainability in mind, featuring water conservation systems, energy-efficient appliances, and natural insulation. Staying in these types of accommodations reduces environmental impact while offering a cozy, luxurious stay.
- Local and Organic Materials: When booking accommodations, look for those that use local materials and organic products to reduce waste and carbon emissions.

2. Green Hotel Certifications
- Energy Efficiency: Hotels and guesthouses with green certifications typically implement energy-

saving initiatives, such as LED lighting, energy-efficient heating and cooling systems, and motion sensors for electricity.
- Waste Reduction: These accommodations also focus on reducing waste through recycling programs, composting, and minimizing single-use plastics.
- Water Conservation: Many eco-friendly hotels in Skopelos use water-saving techniques, such as low-flow faucets and toilets, rainwater harvesting, and gray water recycling for irrigation.

Green Transportation Options
Traveling sustainably in Skopelos also involves minimizing your carbon footprint when moving around the island. Skopelos offers several eco-friendly transportation options for travelers.

1. Walking and Cycling
- Walking: Skopelos is known for its scenic, walkable routes that allow travelers to explore the island at a leisurely pace while reducing pollution. Walking not only reduces your carbon footprint but also provides a more immersive experience of the island's landscapes and culture.
- Cycling: Many areas of Skopelos are accessible by bike, with stunning coastal and countryside cycling routes. Renting a bicycle is a low-impact way to explore the island while enjoying its natural beauty.

Be sure to choose cycling-friendly paths to avoid traffic and ensure safety.

2. Public Transportation and Carpooling
- Public Buses: Skopelos has a reliable public bus system that connects major towns and beaches. Opting for buses reduces the need for private vehicles, which contribute to traffic and pollution. Buses in Skopelos are relatively inexpensive, making them an eco-friendly and budget-conscious choice.
- Carpooling: If you plan to rent a car, consider sharing the vehicle with other travelers. Carpooling not only cuts down on fuel emissions but also allows for social interaction and shared experiences with other visitors.

3. Electric Vehicles and Low-Emission Rentals
- Electric Car Rentals: Some rental agencies in Skopelos offer electric vehicles or low-emission cars. Electric vehicles help reduce greenhouse gas emissions and air pollution while still allowing you the freedom to explore the island.
- Hybrid and Low-Emission Scooters: If you prefer a more adventurous way to travel, opt for hybrid or low-emission scooters. These smaller vehicles consume less fuel than cars, making them a more sustainable choice.

Minimizing Waste and Single-Use Plastics
A significant part of eco-friendly travel is reducing the waste you produce, especially single-use plastics. On an island like Skopelos, where the environment is sensitive, reducing waste is essential to protect its ecosystems.

1. Carry Reusable Items
- Reusable Water Bottles: Instead of buying bottled water, bring a reusable water bottle with you. Skopelos has access to clean drinking water, and many cafes and restaurants are happy to refill your bottle. This simple action can significantly reduce plastic waste.
- Reusable Shopping Bags: Bring reusable shopping bags for groceries and souvenirs. Avoid plastic bags, which can easily end up in the ocean, harming marine life.
- Eco-Friendly Toiletries: Opt for solid toiletries such as bar shampoo and soap instead of plastic-bottled products. Many eco-conscious travelers also carry reusable travel containers for liquids.

2. Say No to Single-Use Plastics
- Plastic-Free Dining: When dining out or grabbing a takeaway, ask for no plastic utensils or straws. Many local restaurants are already shifting toward more sustainable practices by offering compostable or reusable alternatives.

- Beach Waste: Always take your trash with you when visiting Skopelos's beaches, and consider participating in beach clean-ups. Even a small effort to collect litter can make a big difference.

Eco-Friendly Adventures
Skopelos offers countless outdoor adventures that are perfect for eco-conscious travelers, from hiking and snorkeling to wildlife spotting. Choose sustainable activities to help preserve the island's fragile ecosystems.

1. Hiking and Nature Walks
- Marked Trails: Skopelos has a network of hiking trails that allow you to explore the island's forests, hills, and beaches on foot. Stick to marked trails to avoid damaging fragile plants or disturbing wildlife.
- Guided Eco-Tours: Join local guided eco-tours that emphasize environmental education and conservation. These tours provide insight into the island's flora and fauna while supporting local eco-tourism businesses.

2. Snorkeling and Kayaking
- Respect Marine Life: Skopelos is surrounded by rich marine life, but it's important to respect the underwater ecosystem. When snorkeling, avoid touching coral or marine creatures. Choose eco-

friendly sunscreen that doesn't harm the water's biodiversity.
- Non-Motorized Water Sports: Activities like kayaking and paddleboarding have minimal impact on the environment compared to motorized boats. Explore the island's coastline by paddle-powered vessels, which are quieter and kinder to marine life.

Supporting Local and Sustainable Businesses
When you travel, the choices you make about where to eat, shop, and explore can have a positive impact on the local economy and environment. Supporting sustainable businesses is a key aspect of eco-friendly travel.

1. Farm-to-Table Dining
- Local Taverns: Choose restaurants that serve local, organic, and seasonal produce. Many of Skopelos's taverns and restaurants use farm-to-table practices, offering fresh ingredients sourced from nearby farms and fishermen. This not only supports the local economy but also reduces the carbon footprint associated with transporting food.
- Sustainable Seafood: Look for restaurants that serve sustainable seafood. The Northern Sporades, including Skopelos, are known for their fresh fish, but overfishing is a concern. Some taverns offer sustainably caught or farmed fish, ensuring marine populations remain healthy.

2. Buying Local Souvenirs
- Handcrafted Souvenirs: Support local artisans by purchasing handmade crafts and souvenirs. Look for eco-friendly items such as ceramics, woven goods, and organic olive oil. Avoid mass-produced, plastic souvenirs that have little connection to the island's culture.
- Sustainable Craft Markets: Skopelos's markets often feature vendors selling local and sustainable products. Items like organic honey, herbs, and eco-friendly cosmetics make great, low-impact gifts to bring home.

Protecting Natural Habitats and Wildlife
Skopelos's forests, marine parks, and wildlife habitats are delicate and require conscious protection. Respecting these environments ensures their preservation for generations to come.

1. Leave No Trace
- Respect Wildlife: Whether you're hiking in the forests or exploring the waters, be respectful of the wildlife around you. Avoid approaching or feeding animals, as human interaction can disrupt their natural behaviors.
- Take Only Photos: When exploring Skopelos's natural areas, take nothing but photos and leave nothing behind. Picking plants, disturbing rocks, or

taking natural souvenirs can harm the local ecosystem.
- Responsible Camping: If you're camping on Skopelos, be sure to camp only in designated areas and leave no trace of your stay. Bring all waste back with you and avoid disturbing wildlife habitats.

2. Conservation Projects
- Support Marine Conservation: Skopelos is part of the National Marine Park of Alonissos and Northern Sporades, one of the largest marine parks in Europe. By supporting local conservation initiatives, such as adopting a marine species or donating to wildlife protection programs, you contribute to preserving the island's marine life.
- Participate in Clean-Up Activities: Skopelos regularly organizes beach clean-ups and conservation projects. Participating in these activities during your stay is a great way to give back and help protect the island's natural beauty.

Eco-friendly travel is about making conscious choices that benefit both the environment and the local community. From staying in sustainable accommodations to choosing eco-friendly transportation and supporting local businesses, there are many ways to enjoy Skopelos responsibly. By respecting the island's ecosystems, reducing waste, and embracing sustainable activities, you can help preserve the beauty of Skopelos for future generations to experience.

Emergency Contacts And Medical Care in Skopelos

When traveling to a new destination, it's essential to be aware of local emergency services and healthcare options. Although Skopelos is a relatively small and peaceful island, having access to emergency contacts and knowing where to seek medical care can make a significant difference in the event of an emergency.

Emergency Contacts

Skopelos has a range of emergency services that can be contacted if needed. Whether you're dealing with a medical emergency, fire, or need police assistance, the following numbers are important to keep on hand during your trip.

1. General Emergency Number: 112
- 112 is the European Union-wide emergency number, and it connects you to police, fire, and medical services. You can dial 112 from any phone (including mobile phones) even if you don't have a signal from your network provider, and the operators speak English and other languages.

2. Local Emergency Numbers

While 112 can be used for any emergency, the following numbers connect you directly to the specific emergency services in Greece:

- Police: Dial 100 to contact local law enforcement in Skopelos for assistance with accidents, crimes, or any security-related issues.
- Fire Department: Dial 199 in case of fires, forest fires, or related emergencies.
- Ambulance/Medical Emergency: Dial 166 for urgent medical assistance and ambulance services.

3. Coast Guard and Sea Rescue

Since Skopelos is an island with extensive coastline and many travelers engage in water activities, having contact information for the coast guard is vital.

- Coast Guard: Dial 108 for emergency situations at sea, including rescue operations, boat accidents, or any maritime-related emergency.

Medical Care Facilities in Skopelos

Skopelos has basic medical facilities that cater to common health needs, from minor injuries to more serious conditions. For critical health emergencies, patients may need to be transferred to nearby islands or the mainland, where larger hospitals are available.

1. Skopelos Health Center
The primary healthcare facility on the island is the Skopelos Health Center, located in Skopelos Town (Hora). This facility is equipped to handle general medical needs, minor injuries, and emergency first aid.

- Location: Skopelos Town
- Services: General medical care, emergency services, minor surgeries, and first aid treatment.
- Hours: Open 24/7 for emergency situations, with regular outpatient services during working hours.
- Contact: +30 24240 22222 (for general inquiries and appointments)

While the Skopelos Health Center can handle most medical cases, it may not have specialized doctors or advanced medical equipment. For more severe conditions, patients are typically transferred to larger hospitals via ferry or helicopter.

2. Pharmacies
Pharmacies are widespread on Skopelos and are an excellent resource for over-the-counter medications, basic medical supplies, and advice for minor health issues. Pharmacies are located in:

- Skopelos Town: Several pharmacies operate in the main town, providing medications and first aid supplies.

- Glossa: There is also a pharmacy in Glossa, Skopelos's second-largest village, providing similar services.

- Pharmacy Hours: Typically open from morning to evening, but hours may vary. Some pharmacies may offer emergency services after hours (watch for the "night shift" notice on their door).

Serious Medical Emergencies and Transfers

1. Transfers to Nearby Hospitals

For serious medical emergencies that require specialized care, patients are transferred to hospitals on neighboring islands or the mainland. The nearest hospitals are located in:

- Skiathos: The Skiathos Health Center is the closest facility with more extensive services. It's just a ferry ride away from Skopelos.

- Volos: For more serious conditions, patients are often transferred to the General Hospital of Volos on the mainland, which is well-equipped with advanced medical care, specialists, and facilities for major surgeries and critical care.

2. Medical Evacuations

- Helicopter Evacuations: In extreme emergencies, especially life-threatening situations where time is critical, patients may be airlifted by helicopter to larger hospitals on the mainland, typically to Volos or Athens. This service is often coordinated through the Skopelos Health Center or the national emergency line 166.
- Ferry Transfers: In less urgent cases, patients may be transferred via ferry to Skiathos or Volos, depending on the severity of the situation.

Health Insurance and Travel Coverage

Before visiting Skopelos, it's essential to ensure you have adequate travel and health insurance that covers medical expenses and emergency evacuation. Check your insurance policy to confirm:
- Coverage for Medical Treatment: Ensure it covers healthcare costs, including doctor visits, hospital stays, and medications.
- Emergency Evacuations: Verify that your insurance covers the costs of emergency medical transfers, whether by ferry or helicopter.
- Adventure Activities: If you plan on engaging in activities like hiking, snorkeling, or other water sports, make sure your insurance includes coverage for injuries related to these activities.

For EU citizens, a European Health Insurance Card (EHIC) or the updated Global Health Insurance Card (GHIC) provides access to necessary healthcare during temporary stays in Greece. However, additional travel insurance is still recommended.

Tips for Staying Healthy and Safe
- Stay Hydrated: Skopelos can get quite hot in the summer, so make sure to drink plenty of water, especially if you're spending time outdoors.
- Sun Protection: Use sunscreen with high SPF, wear a hat, and reapply sunscreen regularly, particularly if you're swimming or engaging in outdoor activities.
- Insect Bites: Carry insect repellent to prevent mosquito bites, especially during the evening.
- Bring Prescription Medications: Always travel with any necessary prescription medications, as some may be difficult to obtain locally. Carry enough for the duration of your stay, along with a copy of your prescription.
- Emergency Supplies: Pack a small first aid kit with essentials like bandages, antiseptics, and any medications you may need for minor injuries or illnesses.

While Skopelos is a serene and safe destination, knowing where to seek medical help and having emergency contacts on hand ensures that you're prepared for any unexpected health issues or emergencies. With proper planning and awareness, you can enjoy a worry-free stay on this beautiful island.

Chapter 8

ESSENTIAL PLANNING: MAKE THE MOST OF YOUR TRIP

When To Visit: Best Times For Weather And Festivals

Choosing the right time to visit Skopelos can significantly enhance your experience on the island, whether you're seeking pleasant weather or vibrant cultural events. Skopelos enjoys a Mediterranean climate, with distinct seasons that offer unique opportunities for exploration and enjoyment.

Best Times for Weather

Skopelos's climate is characterized by warm, sunny summers and mild winters, making it a year-round destination with varying experiences depending on the season.

1. Spring (April to June)
- Weather: Spring is one of the most delightful times to visit Skopelos. The temperatures range from 15°C to 25°C (59°F to 77°F), providing a pleasant, mild climate perfect for outdoor activities. The island's landscapes are lush and green, with wildflowers in full bloom.
- Activities: Spring is ideal for hiking, exploring the island's natural beauty, and enjoying the quieter beaches. The mild temperatures also make it a great time for cycling and visiting local villages.

2. Summer (July to August)
- Weather: Summer brings warm, sunny weather with temperatures ranging from 25°C to 35°C (77°F to 95°F). The island experiences long daylight hours and minimal rainfall, making it perfect for beach activities and water sports.
- Activities: This is the peak tourist season, so expect lively beaches, bustling towns, and numerous events. It's an excellent time for swimming, sailing, and participating in local festivals. However, it's also the busiest time, so plan accommodations and activities in advance.

3. Autumn (September to October)

- Weather: Autumn offers slightly cooler temperatures ranging from 20°C to 30°C (68°F to 86°F). The weather is still warm, but the crowds thin out, making it a more relaxed time to visit.
- Activities: Enjoy the pleasant weather for sightseeing, hiking, and exploring the island's cultural sites. The sea remains warm enough for swimming, and there are fewer tourists, allowing for a more tranquil experience.

4. Winter (November to March)
- Weather: Winter on Skopelos is mild compared to mainland Europe, with temperatures ranging from 10°C to 15°C (50°F to 59°F). Rainfall is more frequent, and some businesses and accommodations may close for the season.
- Activities: This is the quietest time on the island, ideal for those who prefer solitude and cooler temperatures. It's a good time for off-season travel and experiencing local life without the tourist crowds. However, some outdoor activities and beach visits may be limited due to weather conditions.

Best Times for Festivals

Skopelos is rich in cultural traditions and festivals throughout the year. Participating in these events offers a unique glimpse into local customs and celebrations.

1. Spring Festivals
- Easter Celebrations: Easter is a significant festival in Greece, celebrated with various traditional events on Skopelos. Expect church services, processions, and festive meals featuring local specialties like lamb and tsoureki (Easter bread).
- Skopelos Blossom Festival: Held in April or May, this festival celebrates the island's blooming flowers with local craft stalls, music, and dance performances. It's a great way to experience the island's vibrant springtime atmosphere.

2. Summer Festivals
- Skopelos Music Festival: This annual festival takes place in July and features performances from local and international musicians. The festival includes classical, jazz, and traditional Greek music, held in various venues around the island.
- Panagia (Assumption) Festival: Celebrated on August 15th, this major religious festival is held in honor of the Assumption of the Virgin Mary. It includes church services, processions, and communal feasts, often in the villages and churches dedicated to the Virgin Mary.
- Local Village Fairs: Throughout summer, various villages host their own local fairs with traditional food, music, and dancing. These fairs offer a glimpse into local life and culture.

3. Autumn Festivals
- Harvest Festivals: In September and October, Skopelos celebrates the harvest season with festivals that highlight local produce, including olives, grapes, and wine. These festivals feature traditional music, dance, and food tastings.
- Skopelos Olive Festival: Held in October, this festival focuses on the island's olive oil production. Visitors can learn about olive oil making, participate in tastings, and enjoy local culinary demonstrations.

4. Winter Festivities
- Christmas Celebrations: Skopelos celebrates Christmas with festive decorations, local markets, and special church services. The island's winter atmosphere is calm and charming, with traditional Greek Christmas treats like melomakarona (honey cookies) and kourabiedes (almond cookies).
- New Year's Celebrations: New Year's Eve is marked with local parties and celebrations, including traditional Greek music and dance. On January 1st, St. Basil's Day is celebrated with special church services and the cutting of the Vasilopita (New Year's cake) with a coin hidden inside for good luck.

The best time to visit Skopelos depends on your preferences for weather and cultural experiences. Spring and autumn offer mild temperatures and fewer tourists, making them ideal for a relaxed visit. Summer provides vibrant festivals and excellent beach weather, though it's the busiest time of year. Winter is the quietest season, perfect for those seeking solitude and a more authentic local experience.

Travel Essentials: What To Pack For Skopelos

Packing appropriately for your trip to Skopelos ensures that you're well-prepared for the island's diverse weather conditions, activities, and cultural experiences. Here's a comprehensive packing guide to help you make the most of your visit to this beautiful Greek island.

1. Clothing

Casual Wear

- Lightweight Clothing: Pack breathable, lightweight clothes such as T-shirts, shorts, and sundresses for the warm weather, especially during the summer months.
- Comfortable Footwear: Bring comfortable walking shoes or sandals for exploring the towns

and hiking trails. Consider packing a pair of flip-flops for the beach.

Beachwear
- Swimwear: Pack multiple swimsuits for beach days and swimming. A cover-up or sarong is also handy for walking to and from the beach.
- Beach Towel: A quick-dry beach towel is essential for sunbathing and swimming.

Evening and Formal Wear
- Smart Casual Outfits: For dining out or attending festivals, include a few smart casual outfits. Lightweight dresses or collared shirts and trousers can be suitable for more upscale restaurants and evening events.

Layering Pieces
- Light Jacket or Sweater: Even in summer, evenings can be cooler. A light jacket or sweater will keep you comfortable.
- Rain Jacket: If you're traveling in spring or autumn, a waterproof jacket is useful for unexpected showers.

Activewear
- Hiking Gear: If you plan on hiking, pack appropriate activewear, including moisture-wicking

shirts, durable shorts or pants, and a good pair of hiking shoes.
- Sportswear: For water sports like kayaking or snorkeling, bring swimwear, a rash guard, and any specific gear required for these activities.

2. Accessories
Sun Protection
- Sunscreen: Choose a high-SPF sunscreen to protect your skin from the strong Mediterranean sun.
- Hat: A wide-brimmed hat provides additional sun protection for your face and neck.
- Sunglasses: Polarized sunglasses will help reduce glare and protect your eyes from UV rays.

Beach Essentials
- Beach Bag: A large, waterproof beach bag is useful for carrying your beach gear, snacks, and personal items.
- Snorkel Gear: If you have your own snorkel mask and fins, bring them along. While they can often be rented, having your own gear is more convenient.

Travel Documents
- Passport: Ensure you have your passport or ID card, as you'll need it for travel and identification.
- Travel Insurance: Carry a copy of your travel insurance policy details in case of emergencies.

Electronics
- Camera: A camera or smartphone with a good camera will help you capture the stunning landscapes and memorable moments.
- Chargers and Adapters: Bring the necessary chargers for your devices and a plug adapter if your home country uses a different plug type.

3. Health and Safety Items
First Aid Kit
- Basic Supplies: Include band-aids, antiseptic wipes, pain relievers, and any personal medications you might need.
- Insect Repellent: A mosquito repellent can help protect you from insect bites, especially in warmer months.

Medications
- Prescription Medications: Bring sufficient quantities of any prescription medications you take regularly, along with a copy of your prescription.
- Over-the-Counter Medications: Pack common remedies for issues like headaches, allergies, and digestive problems.

4. Essentials for Exploring
Navigation Aids

- Maps and Guidebooks: While you can use digital maps on your phone, having a physical map or guidebook can be useful for navigating less well-marked areas.
- Travel Apps: Download useful travel apps for navigation, restaurant recommendations, and local information.

Reusable Items
- Water Bottle: A reusable water bottle is important for staying hydrated, especially if you're exploring in the heat.
- Shopping Bags: Bring reusable shopping bags to reduce plastic waste when buying groceries or souvenirs.

5. Cultural Considerations

Respectful Clothing
- Modest Attire: When visiting religious sites or churches, dress modestly. Cover your shoulders and avoid wearing short skirts or shorts.
- Respect Local Customs: Understanding local customs and dressing appropriately shows respect for the island's culture and traditions.

Language Aids
- Phrasebook: If you don't speak Greek, a phrasebook or language app can be helpful for

communicating with locals and navigating the island.

Packing thoughtfully for Skopelos will help ensure a comfortable and enjoyable trip. By bringing the right clothing, accessories, and essentials, you'll be well-prepared to make the most of the island's stunning landscapes, vibrant culture, and diverse activities.

Getting Around: Tips For Renting Vehicles And Public Transit

Navigating Skopelos efficiently involves understanding both vehicle rentals and public transit options. Here are some practical tips to help you get around the island smoothly and enjoy your travels.

Renting Vehicles
1. Types of Vehicles to Consider
- Scooters and Motorbikes: Ideal for exploring the island's narrow roads and reaching remote beaches. They are fuel-efficient and easy to park.
- Cars: A small or compact car is recommended for maneuvering through Skopelos's winding roads and villages. Ensure the car has adequate air conditioning for the warm summer months.
- ATVs: All-terrain vehicles can be a fun option for tackling both paved and unpaved roads, especially if you plan on visiting off-the-beaten-path locations.

2. Booking in Advance
- Pre-Book Online: Reserve your vehicle in advance, especially during peak tourist season (summer months), to ensure availability and potentially better rates.
- Check Reviews: Read reviews of rental companies to gauge their reliability and service quality.

3. Rental Requirements
- Driver's License: Ensure you have a valid driver's license. An international driving permit (IDP) may be required if your license is not in English or Greek.
- Insurance: Confirm that your rental includes insurance coverage. It's also wise to check your travel insurance to see if it covers vehicle rentals.
- Fuel Policy: Understand the fuel policy. Some rentals require you to return the vehicle with a full tank, while others may provide a full tank at pickup.

4. Driving Tips
- Road Conditions: Be prepared for narrow and winding roads. Drive cautiously and be aware of local driving habits.
- Parking: Parking can be limited in popular areas. Look for designated parking spots and avoid parking in restricted zones.

- Local Traffic Laws: Familiarize yourself with local traffic laws and road signs. Wearing seatbelts is mandatory, and mobile phone use while driving is prohibited unless using hands-free devices.

Public Transit

1. Buses
- Local Bus Services: Skopelos has a local bus network connecting major towns and villages. The buses are a cost-effective way to get around, especially if you don't plan on renting a vehicle.
- Bus Schedules: Check the bus schedules in advance, as services can be less frequent during off-peak times. Schedules are usually posted at bus stops or available from the Skopelos Transport Office.
- Tickets: Purchase tickets at bus stations or on the bus, if available. Keep your ticket handy as it may need to be shown during your journey.

2. Taxis
- Availability: Taxis are available throughout Skopelos and can be flagged down or booked in advance. They are a convenient option if you prefer not to drive.
- Fares: Taxi fares are generally metered, but it's a good idea to confirm the estimated cost with the driver before starting your trip. It's also helpful to carry some cash, as not all taxis accept credit cards.

3. Ferries and Boat Services
- Island Connections: Ferries and boat services connect Skopelos with neighboring islands like Skiathos and Alonissos, as well as the mainland. These are useful for island hopping and exploring nearby destinations.
- Booking: For popular routes, book your ferry tickets in advance, especially during the busy summer season. Tickets can often be purchased online or at the ferry port.
- Schedules: Check ferry schedules and plan your trips according to the departure and arrival times. Keep in mind that schedules may vary based on the season and weather conditions.

General Tips

1. Navigation
- Maps and Apps: Use maps or GPS apps to help with navigation. Offline maps can be useful if you're in areas with limited mobile reception.
- Local Advice: Don't hesitate to ask locals for directions or recommendations on the best routes and places to visit.

2. Accessibility
- Accessibility Considerations: If you have mobility issues or require special assistance, check in

advance with rental companies and transit services to ensure they can accommodate your needs.

3. Safety and Security
- Secure Belongings: Keep your belongings secure, especially when using public transport or when parking your rental vehicle. Avoid leaving valuables in plain sight.
- Emergency Contacts: Have contact information for local rental companies, transit services, and emergency services readily available.

Navigating Skopelos can be a delightful experience with the right preparation. Whether you choose to rent a vehicle, use public transit, or combine both methods, understanding your options and planning ahead will ensure a smooth and enjoyable stay on the island.

Important Travel Documents And Insurance

Properly preparing your travel documents and insurance is crucial for a smooth and stress-free visit to Skopelos. Here's a comprehensive guide on what you need to consider for your trip.

Travel Documents

1. Passport and Identification
- Passport: Ensure your passport is valid for at least six months beyond your intended stay. This is a standard requirement for entry into Greece and other Schengen Area countries.
- ID Card: For EU citizens, a national ID card can be used instead of a passport. Ensure it's valid for the duration of your stay.

2. Visa Requirements
- Schengen Visa: Non-EU visitors may require a Schengen visa to enter Greece. Check the visa requirements specific to your nationality and apply well in advance of your trip.
- Visa-Free Travel: Citizens of certain countries, including the US, Canada, Australia, and New Zealand, can enter Greece visa-free for short stays (up to 90 days within a 180-day period). Verify your eligibility before traveling.

3. Travel Itinerary and Accommodation Details
- Itinerary: Keep a copy of your travel itinerary, including flight details, accommodation bookings, and any planned activities. This can be useful for entry and exit checks and for reference during your stay.
- Accommodation Confirmation: Print or save digital copies of your accommodation bookings.

This will be helpful for check-ins and if any issues arise.

4. Proof of Financial Means
- Bank Statements: Some countries may require proof of sufficient funds for the duration of your stay. Bring recent bank statements or proof of income if required for visa applications or entry checks.
- Credit/Debit Cards: Ensure you have accessible credit or debit cards for payments and emergencies. Inform your bank of your travel plans to avoid any issues with card usage abroad.

5. Health Documentation
- Vaccination Records: While not typically required for Greece, it's good practice to carry proof of vaccinations if you have specific health concerns or are traveling from areas with disease outbreaks.
- Medical Prescriptions: If you're bringing prescription medications, carry a copy of your prescriptions and keep medications in their original packaging.

Travel Insurance

1. Coverage Types
- Health Insurance: Ensure your travel insurance includes comprehensive health coverage. This

should cover medical treatment, hospital stays, and emergency evacuations.

- Trip Cancellation: Consider insurance that covers trip cancellation or interruption due to unforeseen events, such as illness or travel disruptions.

- Baggage Loss: Coverage for lost, stolen, or damaged baggage can be useful. Ensure your policy covers the replacement cost of essential items.

- Personal Liability: Insurance that includes personal liability coverage can protect you in case of accidents or damage to property.

2. Choosing Insurance

- Compare Policies: Shop around and compare different insurance policies to find one that best fits your needs. Consider factors such as coverage limits, exclusions, and the claims process.

- Read the Fine Print: Thoroughly read the terms and conditions of your insurance policy. Ensure you understand what is covered and any exclusions or limitations.

3. Emergency Contact Information

- Insurance Provider Contact: Keep contact details for your insurance provider handy in case you need to make a claim or get assistance while abroad.

- Emergency Services: Know the local emergency numbers and procedures in Greece, as well as the contact information for your country's embassy or consulate in Greece.

4. Documentation for Claims
- Keep Receipts: Retain all receipts and documentation related to any medical treatments, travel disruptions, or other incidents. These will be necessary when filing an insurance claim.
- **Claim Forms**: Familiarize yourself with the process for submitting claims and keep any relevant forms or instructions from your insurance provider.

Additional Tips

1. Copies of Important Documents
- Backup Copies: Make photocopies or digital copies of your passport, visa, travel insurance, and other important documents. Keep these copies separate from the originals in case of loss or theft.

2. Contact Information
- Emergency Contacts: Have a list of emergency contacts, including family members, your insurance provider, and the local embassy or consulate.

3. Keep Documents Safe

- Secure Storage: Use a secure method to carry your important documents, such as a money belt or a locked luggage compartment.

Having the right travel documents and insurance in place is crucial for a hassle-free trip to Skopelos. By preparing and organizing these essentials in advance, you can focus on enjoying your time on this beautiful island and handle any unforeseen issues with confidence.

Chapter 9

SAMPLED ITINERARIES FOR EVERY KIND OF TRAVELER

3-Day Itinerary: Quick Getaway Highlights

For a compact yet enriching experience on Skopelos, this 3-day itinerary offers a perfect blend of relaxation, exploration, and local flavor. From picturesque beaches to charming villages.

Day 1: Discovering Skopelos Town

Morning
- Arrival and Check-In: Arrive in Skopelos and check into your accommodation. Choose a centrally located hotel or guesthouse to be close to the main attractions.
- Breakfast at a Local Café: Start your day with a traditional Greek breakfast at a local café. Enjoy items like Greek yogurt with honey, fresh fruits, and pastries.

Midday
- Explore Skopelos Town: Wander through the charming streets of Skopelos Town. Visit the Skopelos Museum to learn about the island's history and culture. Don't miss the picturesque

harbor area, lined with colorful boats and quaint shops.
- Lunch at a Local Taverna: Enjoy a delicious lunch at a traditional taverna. Try local specialties like Skopelitiki Tyri (local cheese pie) or moussaka.

Afternoon
- Panagitsa of Pyrgos: Visit the iconic Panagitsa of Pyrgos church, perched on a hill overlooking the town. The panoramic views of Skopelos Town and the Aegean Sea are stunning.
- Shopping and Souvenirs: Stroll through the narrow streets of Skopelos Town to pick up souvenirs and local crafts. Look for handmade ceramics, olive oil products, and traditional textiles.

Evening
- Dinner at a Seaside Restaurant: Enjoy dinner at a seaside restaurant, where you can savor fresh seafood while watching the sunset. Opt for grilled fish or seafood pasta.
- Evening Stroll: After dinner, take a leisurely walk along the harbor, enjoying the serene evening atmosphere and the illuminated views of the town.

Day 2: Beach Relaxation and Cultural Exploration
Morning

- Breakfast and Beach Time: Have breakfast at your accommodation or a local café. Head to Stafilos Beach, one of the island's most beautiful sandy beaches, for a relaxing morning by the sea.
- Swimming and Sunbathing: Enjoy swimming in the clear turquoise waters and sunbathing on the soft sands.

Midday
- Lunch at a Beachside Bar: Grab a casual lunch at a beachside bar. Enjoy light fare like Greek salad, tzatziki, and grilled meats or fish.
- Explore Glossa Village: In the afternoon, take a short drive or bus ride to Glossa Village, a traditional village known for its charming streets and local architecture. Explore its narrow lanes and enjoy the local atmosphere.

Afternoon
- Visit the Folklore Museum: In Glossa, visit the Folklore Museum to gain insight into the local culture and traditions. The museum features traditional costumes, artifacts, and exhibits on local life.
- Relax at a Local Café: Enjoy a coffee or a refreshing drink at a local café in Glossa, soaking in the tranquil village ambiance.

Evening

- Dinner in Glossa: Have dinner at a local restaurant in Glossa, where you can experience authentic Greek cuisine. Try dishes like kleftiko (slow-cooked lamb) or gemista (stuffed vegetables).
- Return to Skopelos Town: After dinner, return to Skopelos Town for a relaxed evening. Explore more of the town or enjoy a drink at a local bar.

Day 3: Outdoor Adventure and Relaxation
Morning
- Breakfast and Outdoor Adventure: Start with breakfast, then head out for a morning of adventure. Go for a hike along one of Skopelos's scenic trails, such as the Palouki Trail, which offers stunning views of the island's lush landscape and coastline.
- Explore the Monastery of Agios Ioannis Kastri: Visit the Monastery of Agios Ioannis Kastri, a picturesque spot with breathtaking views. It's a great place for photos and to appreciate the island's natural beauty.

Midday
- Lunch at a Scenic Spot: Pack a picnic lunch to enjoy at a scenic spot or return to Skopelos Town for a meal. Opt for fresh, local dishes and enjoy the relaxed atmosphere.
- Afternoon at a Secluded Beach: Spend your afternoon at a less crowded beach, such as Kastani

Beach or Hovolo Beach. These beaches offer crystal-clear waters and a tranquil setting.

Afternoon
- Leisure and Souvenir Shopping: Return to Skopelos Town for some last-minute shopping or relaxation. Pick up any remaining souvenirs and enjoy a final stroll around the town.

Evening
- Farewell Dinner: Enjoy a farewell dinner at a favorite restaurant or try a new place you've been curious about. Reflect on your trip and savor your last meal on the island.
- Evening Walk: Take a final evening walk along the waterfront or through Skopelos Town's charming streets before heading back to your accommodation.

This 3-day itinerary provides a well-rounded experience of Skopelos, combining cultural exploration, beach relaxation, and outdoor adventure. Whether you're drawn to the island's picturesque landscapes, rich history, or delicious cuisine, this quick getaway will offer memorable highlights and a taste of the island's charm.

5-Day Itinerary: Relaxation And Adventure Combo

This 5-day itinerary combines relaxation with adventure, offering a balanced experience of Skopelos's serene beaches, vibrant culture, and thrilling outdoor activities. Enjoy a mix of beach time, local exploration, and scenic hikes, ensuring a well-rounded and memorable visit to the island.

Day 1: Arrival and Exploring Skopelos Town

Morning
- Arrival and Check-In: Arrive in Skopelos and check into your accommodation. Choose a centrally located hotel or guesthouse for easy access to main attractions.
- Breakfast at a Local Café: Start your day with a traditional Greek breakfast. Try Greek yogurt with honey, fresh fruits, and a coffee at a local café.

Midday
- Wander Skopelos Town: Explore the charming streets of Skopelos Town. Visit the Skopelos Museum to understand the island's history and culture.
- Lunch at a Traditional Taverna: Enjoy a leisurely lunch at a traditional taverna. Sample local dishes such as Skopelitiki Tyri (local cheese pie) or grilled calamari.

Afternoon
- Harbor and Shopping: Stroll along the picturesque harbor, enjoy the views, and shop for local crafts and souvenirs. Look for handmade ceramics, olive oil products, and textiles.

Evening
- Dinner with a View: Have dinner at a seaside restaurant with views of the sunset. Opt for fresh seafood or Greek specialties.
- Evening Walk: Take a relaxed walk around Skopelos Town, enjoying the evening ambiance and perhaps a gelato from a local shop.

Day 2: Beach Relaxation and Village Exploration
Morning
- Breakfast and Beach Time: After breakfast, head to Stafilos Beach. Relax on the sandy shores and swim in the clear blue waters.
- Beachside Snack: Grab a light snack or drink at a nearby beach bar.

Midday
- Lunch at a Beachside Eatery: Enjoy a casual lunch at a beachside eatery. Try Greek classics such as tzatziki and souvlaki.

Afternoon

- Explore Glossa Village: Take a short drive or bus ride to Glossa Village. Wander through its charming streets and visit the Folklore Museum.
- Coffee Break: Enjoy a coffee at a local café in Glossa, soaking in the village's serene atmosphere.

Evening
- Dinner in Glossa: Dine at a traditional restaurant in Glossa. Experience authentic Greek cuisine, such as kleftiko (slow-cooked lamb) or gemista (stuffed vegetables).
- Return to Skopelos Town: Head back to Skopelos Town for a relaxed evening. Explore more of the town or enjoy a drink at a local bar.

Day 3: Hiking and Scenic Views

Morning
- Breakfast and Hiking: After breakfast, set out for a hike on the Palouki Trail. This trail offers stunning views of the island's landscape and coastline.
- Visit Monastery of Agios Ioannis Kastri: Hike to the Monastery of Agios Ioannis Kastri for breathtaking panoramic views. It's an excellent spot for photos and appreciating the island's natural beauty.

Midday

- Lunch at a Scenic Spot: Pack a picnic lunch to enjoy at a scenic spot along the trail or return to Skopelos Town for a meal.

Afternoon
- Relaxation: After your hike, spend the afternoon relaxing at a quiet beach such as Hovolo Beach. Enjoy swimming and sunbathing in a more secluded setting.

Evening
- Dinner in Skopelos Town: Return to Skopelos Town for dinner at a favorite restaurant. Try traditional dishes and enjoy the vibrant town atmosphere.
- Evening Entertainment: Consider visiting a local bar or café for live music or entertainment.

Day 4: Water Sports and Island Hopping
Morning
- Breakfast and Water Sports: Start your day with breakfast, then head to a beach offering water sports. Try kayaking or snorkeling at Kastani Beach, known for its clear waters and beautiful surroundings.
- Beachside Brunch: Enjoy a brunch at a beachside café, sampling light bites and refreshing drinks.

Midday

- Island Hopping: Take a ferry or boat trip to explore nearby islands such as Skiathos or Alonissos. Discover their unique attractions and scenic beauty.
- Lunch on the Island: Have lunch at a local restaurant on one of the neighboring islands, experiencing a new culinary scene.

Afternoon
- Continue Exploring: Continue exploring the neighboring island. Visit local landmarks, relax on a beach, or enjoy a leisurely walk.

Evening
- Return to Skopelos: Head back to Skopelos in the evening. Enjoy a relaxed dinner at a local restaurant or café.
- Evening Leisure: Spend your evening enjoying the local nightlife or a quiet stroll through Skopelos Town.

Day 5: Cultural Immersion and Departure
Morning
- Breakfast and Cultural Visit: Enjoy breakfast, then visit The Church of Agios Athanasios and The Monastery of Evangelistria. These sites offer insight into the island's religious and cultural heritage.

- Explore Local Markets: Visit local markets or shops to pick up any last-minute souvenirs and gifts.

Midday
- Lunch and Final Relaxation: Have a final lunch at a favorite spot. Afterward, spend some time relaxing at a nearby beach or café.

Afternoon
- Prepare for Departure: Return to your accommodation to pack and prepare for your departure.
- Farewell Walk: Take a last leisurely walk around Skopelos Town, savoring the final moments of your trip.

Evening
- Departure: Head to the port or airport for your departure, taking with you memories of a delightful combination of relaxation and adventure on Skopelos.

This 5-day itinerary offers a balanced mix of relaxation and adventure, showcasing Skopelos's stunning natural beauty, vibrant culture, and recreational opportunities. Whether you're lounging on pristine beaches, exploring charming villages, or hiking scenic trails, this plan ensures you experience the best of Skopelos in a memorable and enjoyable way.

7-Day Itinerary: In-Depth Exploration Of Skopelos

This 7-day itinerary provides a comprehensive exploration of Skopelos, combining cultural experiences, natural beauty, and adventure. Immerse yourself in the island's rich history, stunning landscapes, and vibrant local life for a truly memorable visit.

Day 1: Arrival and Introduction to Skopelos Town

Morning

- Arrival and Check-In: Arrive in Skopelos and check into your accommodation. Choose a centrally located hotel or guesthouse to have easy access to the town's attractions.
- Breakfast at a Local Café: Enjoy a traditional Greek breakfast. Sample Greek yogurt with honey, fresh fruits, and a strong coffee.

Midday

- Explore Skopelos Town: Start with a leisurely stroll through Skopelos Town. Visit the Skopelos Museum to learn about the island's history and culture.

- Lunch at a Local Taverna: Dine at a traditional taverna. Try local dishes like Skopelitiki Tyri (local cheese pie) and Greek salad.

Afternoon
- Harbor and Shopping: Walk around the picturesque harbor. Browse local shops for souvenirs, including handmade ceramics and traditional textiles.

Evening
- Dinner with a View: Have dinner at a seaside restaurant. Opt for fresh seafood or traditional Greek fare.
- Evening Walk: Take a stroll around Skopelos Town. Enjoy the evening ambiance and perhaps visit a local café for a dessert or a drink.

Day 2: Cultural Exploration and Scenic Views
Morning
- Breakfast and Historical Sites: Start with breakfast, then visit The Church of Agios Athanasios and The Monastery of Evangelistria. Explore these significant cultural and religious sites.
- Panagitsa of Pyrgos: Visit Panagitsa of Pyrgos for stunning views over Skopelos Town and the Aegean Sea.

Midday

- Lunch at a Traditional Restaurant: Enjoy lunch at a traditional restaurant in Skopelos Town. Try a variety of Greek mezes.
- Explore the Old Town: Continue exploring the charming streets of Skopelos Old Town. Visit local artisan shops and enjoy the local architecture.

Afternoon
- Relaxation at a Café: Take a break at a local café. Enjoy coffee and people-watching.

Evening
- Dinner in Skopelos Town: Choose a cozy restaurant in Skopelos Town for dinner. Sample local specialties like kleftiko (slow-cooked lamb) or moussaka.
- Local Entertainment: Consider visiting a bar or café with live music or a cultural performance.

Day 3: Beach Day and Coastal Exploration
Morning
- Breakfast and Beach Time: Have breakfast and head to Stafilos Beach for a relaxing morning. Enjoy the sun and swim in the clear waters.
- Beachside Snack: Grab a snack or drink at a beachside bar.

Midday

- Lunch at a Beachside Eatery: Enjoy a leisurely lunch at a beachside eatery. Try light fare like Greek salad or grilled fish.

Afternoon
- Visit Kastani Beach: Spend your afternoon at Kastani Beach, known for its beautiful scenery and clear waters. Relax and take in the views.

Evening
- Dinner at a Seaside Restaurant: Return to Skopelos Town or a nearby seaside village for dinner. Choose a restaurant with a view of the sunset.
- Evening Leisure: Relax after dinner with a walk along the waterfront or a visit to a local café.

Day 4: Hiking and Monastery Visits
Morning
- Breakfast and Hiking: After breakfast, embark on a hike along the Palouki Trail. Enjoy stunning views of the island's lush landscape and coastline.
- Monastery of Agios Ioannis Kastri: Visit the Monastery of Agios Ioannis Kastri during your hike. The panoramic views from here are breathtaking.

Midday

- Picnic Lunch: Pack a picnic lunch to enjoy at a scenic spot along the trail or return to Skopelos Town.

Afternoon
- Relaxation at a Beach: After your hike, head to a quieter beach like Hovolo Beach for relaxation and a swim.

Evening
- Dinner at a Local Taverna: Dine at a traditional taverna in Skopelos Town. Try a variety of local dishes.
- Evening Stroll: Take a stroll through Skopelos Town, enjoying the evening ambiance.

Day 5: Glossa Village and Local Culture
Morning
- Breakfast and Trip to Glossa: Enjoy breakfast and then take a drive or bus ride to Glossa Village. Explore its traditional streets and local architecture.
- Visit the Folklore Museum: Visit the Folklore Museum in Glossa to learn more about local customs and traditions.

Midday
- Lunch in Glossa: Have lunch at a traditional restaurant in Glossa. Experience local flavors and specialties.

- Relax at a Café: Enjoy a coffee break at a local café in Glossa.

Afternoon
- Return to Skopelos Town: Head back to Skopelos Town in the afternoon. Spend some time shopping or relaxing at a local café.

Evening
- Dinner and Nightlife: Enjoy dinner at a restaurant in Skopelos Town. Explore the local nightlife with a visit to a bar or café for drinks and entertainment.

Day 6: Water Sports and Island Hopping
Morning
- Breakfast and Water Sports: Start with breakfast, then head to a beach offering water sports. Try kayaking, snorkeling, or sailing at Kastani Beach.
- Beachside Brunch: Enjoy brunch at a beachside bar or café.

Midday
- Island Hopping: Take a ferry or boat trip to neighboring islands such as Skiathos or Alonissos. Explore their unique attractions and scenic beauty.
- Lunch on the Island: Have lunch at a local restaurant on one of the neighboring islands.

Afternoon

- Continued Exploration: Spend the afternoon exploring the neighboring island. Relax on its beaches or visit local landmarks.

Evening
- Return to Skopelos: Head back to Skopelos in the evening. Enjoy a relaxed dinner at a favorite restaurant or try a new place.

Day 7: Relaxation and Departure
Morning
- Breakfast and Final Relaxation: Enjoy your last breakfast on the island. Spend the morning relaxing at your favorite beach or café.
- Final Shopping: Visit local markets or shops to pick up any final souvenirs or gifts.

Midday
- Lunch and Packing: Have a final lunch at a favorite spot. Return to your accommodation to pack and prepare for departure.

Afternoon
- Departure Preparation: Head to the port or airport for your departure. Make sure you have all your belongings and travel documents.

Evening

- Departure: Depart from Skopelos with cherished memories of a comprehensive exploration of the island.

This 7-day itinerary offers a thorough exploration of Skopelos, combining cultural experiences, scenic beauty, and adventure. From relaxing on stunning beaches to hiking scenic trails and exploring charming villages, this plan ensures you experience the island's diverse offerings and enjoy a memorable and enriching visit.

Hidden Gems: Off-the-beaten-path Adventures

Skopelos, renowned for its stunning beaches and charming towns, also boasts hidden gems that offer unique and memorable experiences away from the usual tourist spots. For those seeking off-the-beaten-path adventures, here are some of the island's lesser-known treasures.

1. Pefkias Forest and Waterfall
Description
- Nestled in the lush Pefkias Forest, this serene area is a hidden gem for nature lovers. The forest is filled with pine trees, wildflowers, and a peaceful

atmosphere, offering a refreshing escape from the more frequented spots.

Adventure

- Hiking: Explore the forest trails leading to a picturesque waterfall. The trail is relatively easy, making it accessible for all skill levels.
- Picnic: Enjoy a picnic by the waterfall, surrounded by the tranquil sounds of nature.

2. Agios Ioannis Beach

Description

- This secluded beach is tucked away from the more popular spots, offering pristine sands and crystal-clear waters. It's an ideal spot for those looking to escape the crowds.

Adventure

- Swimming and Relaxation: Enjoy a quiet day sunbathing and swimming in the calm waters. The lack of crowds ensures a peaceful experience.
- Picnic: Bring a packed lunch and enjoy a secluded beach picnic with breathtaking views.

3. Lazarou Monastery

Description

- An ancient and lesser-visited monastery, Lazarou Monastery is perched on a hill, offering panoramic views of the island and the Aegean Sea. Its historical significance and tranquil setting make it a unique visit.

Adventure
- Exploration: Wander through the monastery grounds and explore the old chapels and religious artifacts.
- **Photography: Capture stunning panoramic views of the surrounding landscape and sea.

4. Kastani Beach at Sunset
Description
- While Kastani Beach is known, visiting it at sunset reveals a different, more magical side of this popular spot. The golden hues of the setting sun transform the beach into a stunning visual experience.

Adventure
- Sunset Viewing: Arrive in the late afternoon and find a spot on the beach to watch the sunset. The changing colors over the sea create a mesmerizing backdrop.
- Evening Swim: Enjoy a tranquil swim as the sun sets, with the beach almost entirely to yourself.

5. Village
Description

- This charming fishing village is often overlooked by tourists. Agnondas offers a quaint and authentic Greek village experience with its small harbor and traditional architecture.

Adventure
- Stroll and Explore: Wander through the village streets, visit local shops, and enjoy the laid-back atmosphere.
- Seafood Dining: Dine at a local taverna specializing in fresh seafood. The harbor views and authentic cuisine make for a delightful experience.

6. The Skopelos Olive Oil Museum
Description
- Located in a traditional olive oil mill, this museum offers insight into the island's olive oil production. It's a hidden gem for those interested in local traditions and culinary heritage.

Adventure
- Museum Tour: Take a guided tour to learn about the history and process of olive oil production. Enjoy tasting sessions and explore the exhibits.
- Cooking Workshop: Participate in a cooking workshop, where you can use freshly made olive oil in traditional Greek recipes.

---

7. Glysteri Beach
Description
- A lesser-known beach, Glysteri offers a more tranquil experience compared to other popular spots. Its clear waters and peaceful setting are perfect for relaxation.

Adventure
- Beach Day: Spend the day lounging on the beach, swimming, and enjoying the serene environment.
- Snorkeling: The clear waters are ideal for snorkeling, revealing the vibrant underwater life of Skopelos.

8. Mikros Mourtias Beach
Description
- This hidden beach, accessible only by a short hike or boat, is known for its secluded location and beautiful scenery. It's a perfect spot for those looking for privacy and natural beauty.

Adventure
- **Hiking and Swimming**: Reach the beach via a scenic hike or by boat. Enjoy the solitude and natural beauty of the area.
- **Relaxation**: Spend your time sunbathing and swimming in the clear waters, surrounded by nature.

9. The Old Olive Grove

Description
- This ancient olive grove, located on the outskirts of Skopelos Town, offers a glimpse into traditional agricultural practices. The grove is an off-the-beaten-path location with historical and cultural significance.

Adventure
- Exploration: Walk through the old olive trees and learn about the traditional methods of olive cultivation.
- Photography: Capture the picturesque scenes of the ancient grove and the surrounding countryside.

10. Paleo Kastro (Old Castle)

Description
- The ruins of the old castle offer a historical adventure and stunning panoramic views. It's a lesser-visited site that provides a sense of history and isolation.

Adventure
- Explore the Ruins: Wander through the ancient ruins and imagine the history of the site.
- Viewpoints: Climb to the highest points for breathtaking views of the island and the sea.

Skopelos offers numerous hidden gems that provide unique and off-the-beaten-path adventures. From secluded beaches and ancient monasteries to tranquil villages and historical sites, these lesser-known spots allow for a more intimate and personal experience of the island. Whether you're seeking natural beauty, cultural insights, or peaceful relaxation, these hidden gems are sure to enhance your visit to Skopelos.

Chapter 10

ICONIC LANDMARKS AND MUST-SEE ATTRACTIONS

Agios Loannis Chapel: The Mamma Mia! Church

The Agios Ioannis Chapel, famously known as the "Mamma Mia! Church," is one of Skopelos's most iconic landmarks. Perched dramatically on a rocky outcrop overlooking the Aegean Sea, this charming chapel gained worldwide fame as a filming location for the popular movie "Mamma Mia!" It is a must-visit for both fans of the film and those seeking to experience one of Skopelos's most picturesque spots.

Historical and Cultural Significance
- Architectural Charm: The chapel, dedicated to Saint John (Agios Ioannis), is a traditional Greek Orthodox structure. It features classic whitewashed walls and a simple, elegant bell tower, embodying the quintessential Greek island aesthetic.
- Religious Importance: While the chapel itself is a site of religious significance, its serene location and historical architecture also reflect the island's rich cultural heritage.

Visit Experience
- Scenic Location: The chapel is set on a rugged rock formation at the edge of the sea, providing breathtaking panoramic views of the surrounding coastline and the Aegean waters. The striking location adds to its appeal and makes it a popular spot for photographers.
- Filming Location: The chapel gained international fame as a key filming location for the 2008 film "Mamma Mia!" starring Meryl Streep and Pierce Brosnan. The stunning scenery and dramatic setting played a significant role in the film's visual appeal, drawing movie fans from around the world.

Getting There
- Access: The chapel is accessible via a steep and winding path that leads from the nearest village,

Glossa. The hike is relatively short but can be challenging due to its incline.

- Transportation: Visitors can reach Glossa by car or local bus, and from there, it's a scenic walk or drive to the chapel. Many visitors choose to hire a local taxi or guided tour for a more convenient journey.

Things to Do
- Explore the Chapel: Take time to admire the simple yet beautiful interior of the chapel, which features traditional religious icons and artifacts.
- Photography: Capture stunning photographs of the chapel against the backdrop of the sea and rugged cliffs. The location offers spectacular opportunities for sunset photography.
- Picnic and Relaxation: Bring a picnic to enjoy on the nearby rocks or in the surrounding area. The peaceful setting is perfect for a relaxing break.

Tips for Visitors
- Wear Comfortable Shoes: The path to the chapel can be uneven and steep, so comfortable walking shoes are essential.
- Check Opening Hours: While the chapel is usually open to visitors, it's a good idea to check local information for any specific opening hours or restrictions, especially if you're visiting during a religious service.

- Respect Local Customs: As a functioning religious site, visitors should dress modestly and be respectful of local customs and practices.

Nearby Attractions
- Glossa Village: Explore the charming village of Glossa, known for its traditional Greek architecture, local shops, and quaint cafes.
- Other Beaches: Enjoy nearby beaches such as Stafilos and Velanio, which offer opportunities for relaxation and swimming.

The Agios Ioannis Chapel, or "Mamma Mia! Church," is a captivating landmark that beautifully combines natural beauty with cultural and cinematic significance. Its dramatic setting and historical charm make it a highlight of any visit to Skopelos, offering a unique experience for both movie enthusiasts and travelers seeking to explore the island's hidden treasures.

Skopelos Old Town: Cobblestone Streets And Historic Charm

Skopelos Old Town is a captivating destination that embodies the island's rich cultural heritage and timeless beauty. With its labyrinth of cobblestone streets, traditional architecture, and charming atmosphere, it stands as one of Skopelos's most iconic landmarks. This historical district offers visitors a delightful journey back in time, providing a glimpse into the island's storied past and vibrant present.

Historical and Cultural Significance
- Architectural Heritage: The Old Town is characterized by its well-preserved traditional Greek architecture. Whitewashed buildings with blue shutters, terracotta roofs, and quaint courtyards

reflect the classic island style that has remained largely unchanged over the centuries.

- Cultural Hub: The area is a cultural and historical hub, where traditional Greek customs and lifestyles are still very much alive. It serves as a living museum, showcasing the island's history through its architecture, shops, and daily life.

Visit Experience
- Wandering the Streets: The narrow, winding cobblestone streets of Skopelos Old Town are perfect for leisurely exploration. Stroll through the charming alleys, discovering hidden squares, colorful bougainvillea, and picturesque homes.
- Historical Landmarks: Along your walk, you'll encounter several historical landmarks, including the Skopelos Museum, housed in a traditional mansion, and various old churches such as Agios Nikolaos and Agios Konstantinos.

Activities and Attractions
- Shopping: Browse local shops and boutiques for unique souvenirs, handmade crafts, and traditional Greek products. Look for items like ceramics, textiles, and local delicacies.
- Dining: Enjoy a meal at one of the Old Town's traditional tavernas or cafes. Sample local specialties while sitting in charming courtyards or with views of the bustling streets.

- Photography: Capture the essence of Skopelos Old Town through your lens. The interplay of light on the cobblestone streets and the vibrant colors of the buildings and flowers make for stunning photographs.

Getting There
- Location: The Old Town is centrally located and easily accessible from most accommodations on the island. It is a short walk from the harbor and other central areas.
- Transportation: Although walking is the best way to explore the Old Town due to its narrow streets, you can also use local taxis or scooters for access to nearby areas.

Tips for Visitors
- Wear Comfortable Shoes: The cobblestone streets can be uneven, so comfortable walking shoes are recommended for exploring the area.
- Stay Hydrated: During the summer months, it's important to stay hydrated as you explore the town. Bring a water bottle and take breaks in the shaded areas of cafes or shops.
-Respect Local Customs: As the Old Town is a residential area, be mindful of local customs and quiet spaces. Respect the privacy of residents while enjoying your visit.

Nearby Attractions

- Skopelos Harbor: Just a short walk from the Old Town, the harbor offers a picturesque setting with waterfront cafes and shops.

- Pefkias Forest: For a nature break, head to Pefkias Forest, located not far from the Old Town. It offers scenic trails and a serene environment for relaxation.

Skopelos Old Town is a treasure trove of historical and cultural experiences. Its cobblestone streets, traditional architecture, and vibrant atmosphere provide an authentic glimpse into the island's past and present. Whether you're wandering through its charming alleys, enjoying local cuisine, or capturing the beauty of its historic buildings, Skopelos Old Town is an essential highlight of any visit to the island.

The Venetian Castle: Panoramic Island Views

The Venetian Castle, or Kastro, is one of Skopelos's most iconic landmarks, offering visitors a compelling blend of history and stunning panoramic views. Perched high on a hill overlooking Skopelos Town and the Aegean Sea, this historic fortress stands as a testament to the island's rich past and strategic importance.

Historical and Cultural Significance
- Historical Background: The Venetian Castle was constructed during the 13th century when Skopelos was under Venetian control. Its purpose was to protect the island from pirate attacks and to assert Venetian influence over the region. The castle played a crucial role in the island's defense and administration during this period.

- Architectural Features: The castle's architecture reflects Venetian military design, characterized by robust stone walls, defensive towers, and strategic positioning. The remains of the castle offer insights into medieval fortification techniques and the historical significance of the Venetian era on the island.

Visit Experience
- Panoramic Views: One of the main attractions of the Venetian Castle is the breathtaking panoramic views it offers. From the castle's elevated position, visitors can enjoy sweeping vistas of Skopelos Town, the surrounding countryside, and the Aegean Sea. The views are particularly stunning at sunrise and sunset.
- Exploration: Wander through the castle's ruins, including the remnants of its defensive walls, towers, and gatehouse. The site provides a fascinating glimpse into medieval life and military architecture.

Activities and Attractions
- Photography: The Venetian Castle offers numerous opportunities for photography. Capture the dramatic views of the island and the sea, as well as the intricate details of the castle's stonework and ruins.

- Historical Insights: Learn about the castle's history and its role in Skopelos's past through informational signs and local guides. The site's historical context adds depth to your visit.
- Relaxation: Take time to relax on the castle's grounds and enjoy the serene atmosphere. The elevated location provides a peaceful escape with panoramic scenery.

Getting There
- Access: The castle is located on a hill above Skopelos Town. The climb to the castle involves a steep but manageable hike, which takes approximately 15-20 minutes from the town center. The path is well-trodden, but comfortable walking shoes are recommended.
- Transportation: While walking is the primary way to reach the castle, local taxis or guided tours may be available for those seeking a more convenient option.

Tips for Visitors
- Wear Comfortable Shoes: The path to the castle can be steep and uneven, so sturdy walking shoes are essential.
- Bring Water and Snacks: It's a good idea to bring water and a light snack, especially if you plan to spend time exploring the site.

- Check Weather Conditions: The castle is best visited on a clear day to fully appreciate the panoramic views. Check the weather forecast before heading up to ensure optimal visibility.

Nearby Attractions
- Skopelos Town: Explore the charming streets of Skopelos Town before or after your visit to the castle. Enjoy local shops, cafes, and restaurants.
- Agios Ioannis Chapel: Located nearby, the Agios Ioannis Chapel, also known as the "Mamma Mia! Church," offers another stunning viewpoint and is worth a visit.

The Venetian Castle is a must-visit landmark on Skopelos, offering a captivating blend of historical significance and natural beauty. Its strategic location provides spectacular panoramic views, making it an ideal spot for both history enthusiasts and those seeking stunning vistas. A visit to the Venetian Castle allows for a deep connection with Skopelos's rich past while enjoying one of the island's most breathtaking landscapes.

Monasteries Of Skopelos: Peaceful Sanctuaries In The Hills

Skopelos is home to several picturesque monasteries that dot the hills and mountains of the island. These serene sanctuaries offer a unique glimpse into the island's spiritual and cultural heritage. Each monastery provides a tranquil retreat away from the hustle and bustle, featuring stunning natural surroundings, historic architecture, and a deep sense of peace.

Monasteries to Visit

1. Monastery of Agios Ioannis Prodromos
   - Location: Nestled in the northern part of Skopelos, this monastery is set on a hill surrounded by lush vegetation.
   - Features: Known for its ancient architecture and religious significance, the monastery is a key site for local festivals and spiritual retreats. The grounds

offer sweeping views of the island and the Aegean Sea.

- Experience: Wander through the monastery's courtyards, admire the historic frescoes, and attend a local religious service if available.

2. Monastery of Panagia Evangelistria
- Location: Situated near Skopelos Town, this monastery is easily accessible and offers a peaceful escape close to the island's main attractions.
- Features: The monastery is renowned for its beautiful iconography and serene garden. It plays an important role in the local community, hosting various religious and cultural events throughout the year.
- Experience: Explore the monastery's interior, which features intricate icons and religious artifacts, and enjoy the tranquil gardens.

3. Monastery of Agios Riginos
- Location: Located on a hill overlooking the southern part of the island, this monastery provides spectacular views and a sense of isolation.
- Features: Agios Riginos is known for its historical significance and well-preserved architecture. The monastery's location offers a peaceful retreat amidst natural beauty.
- Experience: Visit the monastery to experience its calm atmosphere and scenic views. Take a quiet

moment to reflect and enjoy the surrounding landscape.

4. Monastery of Agios Georgios
  - Location: Perched on a hillside, this monastery is surrounded by olive groves and offers panoramic views of the island's countryside.
  - Features: The monastery is notable for its historic significance and the traditional architecture of its buildings. It serves as a center for local religious practices and community gatherings.
  - Experience: Explore the monastery's grounds, admire the traditional architecture, and take in the expansive views of the surrounding landscape.

Visit Experience
- Tranquility: Each monastery provides a peaceful environment perfect for reflection and meditation. The serene settings and spiritual ambiance offer a respite from the more tourist-heavy areas of the island.
- Cultural Insight: Visiting these monasteries provides insight into the religious and cultural traditions of Skopelos. The monasteries often have small museums or displays showcasing religious artifacts and historical items.
- Natural Beauty: The monasteries are set amidst stunning natural landscapes, including hills, forests,

and coastal views. The combination of spiritual and natural beauty makes for a memorable visit.

Getting There
- Access: Most monasteries are accessible by car or scooter. Some may require a short hike or walk from the nearest road or parking area.
- Transportation: Renting a vehicle or joining a guided tour can make visiting multiple monasteries easier. Local taxis may also be an option for reaching more remote locations.

Tips for Visitors
- Dress Modestly: As these are religious sites, visitors should dress modestly. Covering shoulders and knees is generally expected.
- Respect Quietude: Maintain a respectful silence and demeanor while on the monastery grounds, as these are places of worship and reflection.
- Check Opening Hours: Monasteries may have specific opening hours and may be closed during religious services or events. It's a good idea to check in advance.

Nearby Attractions
- Skopelos Town: Explore the town's historical and cultural sites before or after visiting the monasteries.

- Beaches: Relax on nearby beaches like Stafilos or Velanio after a day of exploring the monasteries.

The monasteries of Skopelos offer more than just historical and architectural interest; they provide serene retreats that allow visitors to connect with the island's spiritual heritage. With their stunning locations, peaceful environments, and cultural significance, these monasteries are essential stops for those seeking a deeper understanding of Skopelos's unique charm and tranquility.

Kastani Beach And Panormos: Cinematic Beaches To Visit

Skopelos is renowned for its stunning beaches, with Kastani Beach and Panormos Beach standing out as two of the island's most iconic and picturesque coastal destinations. Both beaches are celebrated for their natural beauty and cinematic appeal, making them must-visit attractions for travelers seeking unforgettable seaside experiences.

Kastani Beach

- Description: Kastani Beach is often hailed as one of Skopelos's most beautiful and photogenic beaches. Its pristine sands, crystal-clear waters, and dramatic backdrop of rocky cliffs and lush pine trees create a breathtaking setting.

- Cinematic Appeal: Kastani Beach gained fame as one of the primary filming locations for the 2008 movie "Mamma Mia!" The beach's stunning scenery and idyllic setting were prominently featured in several key scenes, attracting fans of the film from around the world.

- Activities:
  - Sunbathing and Swimming: Relax on the golden sands or take a refreshing swim in the clear, turquoise waters.
  - Beach Bar: Enjoy drinks and light snacks at the beach bar, which offers a great spot to unwind while taking in the beautiful surroundings.
  - Photography: Capture the picturesque views of the beach, cliffs, and sea, especially during the golden hours of sunrise and sunset.

- Getting There: Kastani Beach is accessible by car or scooter, with parking available near the beach. It is a short drive from Skopelos Town and well-signposted.

Panormos Beach
- Description: Panormos Beach is another gem on Skopelos, known for its serene atmosphere and stunning natural beauty. The beach is characterized by its fine sand, gentle waves, and surrounding lush greenery, creating a tranquil and picturesque environment.

- Cinematic Appeal: Panormos Beach also featured prominently in "Mamma Mia!" The beach's stunning scenery and calm waters made it an ideal location for some of the film's most memorable scenes.

- Activities:
  - Swimming and Relaxation: Enjoy a relaxing day by the sea, swimming in the clear waters and lounging on the soft sand.
  - Kayaking and Snorkeling: The calm and clear waters are perfect for kayaking and snorkeling, allowing you to explore the underwater world.
  - Dining: Visit nearby tavernas and cafes for a taste of local cuisine with views of the beach and sea.

- Getting There: Panormos Beach is located a short drive from Skopelos Town. It is accessible by car, scooter, or local transport, with ample parking available.

Why Visit These Beaches?
- Scenic Beauty: Both Kastani and Panormos Beaches offer breathtaking views and picturesque landscapes that capture the essence of Skopelos's natural beauty. Their clear waters and scenic surroundings provide a perfect backdrop for relaxation and recreation.

- Cinematic Experience: For fans of "Mamma Mia!" visiting these beaches offers a unique opportunity to experience the locations featured in the film. The familiarity of the settings combined with their natural beauty makes for a memorable visit.

- Relaxation and Recreation: Whether you're looking to unwind on the sandy shores, swim in crystal-clear waters, or engage in water sports, these beaches provide a range of activities to suit every preference.

Nearby Attractions
- Skopelos Town: Explore the charming town with its historic sites, shops, and cafes.

- Other Beaches: Consider visiting nearby beaches such as Stafilos and Velanio for more coastal experiences.

Kastani Beach and Panormos Beach are quintessential Skopelos destinations that offer not only stunning natural beauty but also a touch of cinematic magic. Whether you're a movie fan, a beach lover, or simply seeking a beautiful spot to relax, these beaches provide an unforgettable experience that captures the essence of Skopelos's coastal allure.

Chapter 11

WHAT NOT TO DO: AVOID THESE COMMON PITFALLS

Overcrowded Spots: Alternatives To Tourist Traps

While Skopelos offers many popular attractions and picturesque spots, some can become crowded, particularly during peak tourist seasons. To ensure a more relaxed and enjoyable experience, it's helpful to know which areas to avoid and explore alternative destinations that capture the island's charm without the crowds.

Overcrowded Spots to Avoid
1. Main Beaches in Peak Season

- Issue: Popular beaches like Kastani Beach and Panormos Beach can become extremely crowded, especially in July and August. The influx of visitors can lead to difficulty finding space and reduced enjoyment.

- Alternative: Explore less frequented beaches such as Agios Ioannis or Kira Panagia, which offer similar natural beauty with fewer crowds.

2. Skopelos Town During High Tourist Season
- Issue: The town's central areas, including the waterfront and main shopping streets, can become congested, making it challenging to enjoy leisurely walks and dining.

- Alternative: Visit the Old Town early in the morning or late in the evening to avoid peak crowds. Alternatively, explore Glossa Village or Neo Klima, which provide a more tranquil experience.

3. Popular Dining Spots at Peak Hours
- Issue: Well-known restaurants and tavernas in Skopelos Town may experience long waits and overcrowded conditions during peak meal times.

- Alternative: Seek out dining options in less tourist-heavy areas or visit during off-peak hours. Consider dining in Ano Skopelos or Pefki, where you can find local eateries with a more relaxed atmosphere.

Alternative Recommendations
1. Hidden Beaches
   - Agios Riginos: A secluded beach offering a serene environment and stunning views. Its remote location ensures fewer visitors.
   - Milia Beach: Known for its tranquil waters and natural beauty, this beach is less crowded and ideal for relaxation.

2. Quiet Villages
   - Glossa: A charming village with traditional Greek architecture and a slower pace of life. Explore its narrow streets, enjoy local cafes, and experience authentic Greek culture.
   - Neo Klima (Elios): A small coastal village with beautiful views and fewer tourists. It provides a peaceful escape and local dining options.

3. Scenic Hikes and Nature Trails
   - Pefkias Forest: Located near the town, this forest offers scenic walking trails and a peaceful retreat into nature.
   - Mamma Mia! Hiking Trail: Follow trails that lead to filming locations and lesser-known scenic spots on the island, away from the main tourist areas.

4. Local Markets and Artisan Shops

- Local Markets: Visit markets in smaller villages where you can find local produce, crafts, and souvenirs without the crowds found in central Skopelos Town.
- Artisan Shops: Explore shops in quieter parts of the island for unique handcrafted items and local goods.

Tips for Avoiding Crowds
- Travel Off-Peak: If possible, visit Skopelos during the shoulder seasons of late spring or early autumn to avoid the busiest times.
- Explore Early or Late: Visiting popular spots early in the morning or later in the afternoon can help you avoid the peak crowds.
- Use Local Insights: Seek recommendations from locals for hidden gems and less crowded spots to explore.

By avoiding the overcrowded spots and opting for less touristy alternatives, you can experience the true essence of Skopelos in a more relaxed and enjoyable manner. Embrace the island's hidden treasures and tranquil settings to make the most of your visit while avoiding the pitfalls of tourist traps.

Cultural Missteps: What's Considered Rude In Greece

When visiting Greece, being aware of local customs and etiquette can greatly enhance your travel experience and ensure respectful interactions with locals. Greek culture is rich and diverse, with specific norms and behaviors that are important to observe.

Common Cultural Missteps

1. Inappropriate Dress Codes
 - Issue: Wearing revealing clothing in religious sites such as churches and monasteries is considered disrespectful.
 - Avoidance: Dress modestly when visiting religious sites. Cover shoulders and knees, and remove hats when entering churches. Casual yet respectful attire is recommended for everyday activities.

2. Disrespecting Local Customs
 - Issue: Ignoring or disrespecting local customs, such as the traditional Greek greeting and etiquette, can be seen as rude.
 - Avoidance: Greet people with a warm handshake or, among friends, a kiss on both cheeks. Be polite and show appreciation for local customs and traditions.

3. Tipping Etiquette
- Issue: While tipping is appreciated, excessive or insufficient tipping can be awkward. Not tipping at all can also be considered impolite, especially in restaurants and cafes.
- Avoidance: In restaurants, it's customary to leave a tip of around 5-10% of the bill. For other services like taxis or hotel staff, rounding up the fare or giving a small tip is appreciated.

4. Inappropriate Table Manners
- Issue: Certain table manners are important in Greek dining culture. Speaking with your mouth full or making loud noises at the table can be seen as impolite.
- Avoidance: Wait until everyone is served before starting your meal, and avoid discussing controversial topics at the table. Eating with your hands, unless specifically appropriate (like with certain street foods), is generally avoided.

5. Public Displays of Affection
- Issue: Excessive public displays of affection, especially in conservative areas, can be considered inappropriate.
- Avoidance: While holding hands is common, keep more intimate displays of affection private. Show respect for local norms, especially in smaller towns and rural areas.

6. Pointing and Gestures
- Issue: Certain hand gestures or body language can be interpreted differently and may be seen as offensive.
- Avoidance: Avoid pointing directly at people, which can be perceived as rude. Be mindful of gestures; for example, the "OK" sign can sometimes have negative connotations in Greece.

7. Talking Loudly
- Issue: Speaking loudly or drawing excessive attention in public places can be considered rude or disruptive.
- Avoidance: Maintain a moderate tone of voice and be conscious of your surroundings. Respect the local norm of quieter public behavior.

General Etiquette Tips
- Politeness: Greek people value politeness and good manners. Simple phrases such as "Kaliméra" (Good morning) and "Efcharistó" (Thank you) go a long way in making a positive impression.
- Respect for Elders: Show respect to older individuals by offering them your seat if needed and listening attentively during conversations.
- Hospitality: Greeks are known for their hospitality. If invited into someone's home, bring a

small gift like flowers or a bottle of wine as a gesture of appreciation.

Understanding and respecting Greek cultural norms will not only help you avoid potential faux pas but also enrich your travel experience. By being aware of what is considered rude and adapting your behavior accordingly, you'll demonstrate respect for local customs and build positive relationships with the people you encounter during your visit to Greece.

Skipping Local: Why You Should Support Skopelos Business

Supporting local businesses in Skopelos offers numerous benefits to both visitors and the community. By choosing to spend your money at locally-owned shops, restaurants, and services, you contribute to the island's economy, preserve its unique character, and enhance your own travel experience. Here's why supporting local businesses in Skopelos is a choice that benefits everyone involved.

1. Economic Benefits
- Boosting the Local Economy: Money spent at local businesses stays within the community, helping to create and sustain jobs and stimulate

economic growth. Local entrepreneurs often reinvest their earnings into the island, supporting further development and improving community services.

- Reducing Economic Leakage: When you support local businesses, less money is sent out of the island. This helps ensure that more of your spending directly benefits the Skopelos community rather than larger, international chains.

2. Authentic Experience

- Unique Products and Services: Local businesses often offer products and services that are unique to Skopelos, providing a more authentic and memorable travel experience. From handmade crafts and local delicacies to traditional Greek experiences, you'll find offerings that reflect the island's cultural heritage.

- Personalized Service: Local businesses are known for their personalized customer service. Shop owners, restaurateurs, and service providers take pride in offering a warm, welcoming atmosphere and are often eager to share their local knowledge and recommendations.

3. Preserving Local Character

- Maintaining Skopelos's Charm: By supporting local businesses, you help preserve the island's unique character and charm. Large, impersonal

chains can sometimes dilute the local culture, while independent businesses contribute to Skopelos's distinctive atmosphere and authenticity.
- Encouraging Sustainable Practices: Many local businesses prioritize sustainable and eco-friendly practices. Supporting these businesses helps promote environmental responsibility and contributes to the preservation of Skopelos's natural beauty.

4. Community Support
- Strengthening Community Ties: Local businesses often play an active role in their communities, sponsoring events, supporting local charities, and participating in cultural activities. Your support helps strengthen these community connections and encourages a vibrant, engaged local society.
- Building Relationships: Engaging with local business owners and residents fosters a sense of connection and mutual respect. You'll have the opportunity to make new friends, learn about local traditions, and gain insights into everyday life on the island.

5. Enhancing Your Travel Experience
- Discover Hidden Gems: Local businesses often have insider knowledge about the best spots to visit, eat, and shop. By supporting them, you gain access

to hidden gems and off-the-beaten-path attractions that you might not find in tourist guides.

- Creating Lasting Memories: The personalized touch and unique offerings of local businesses contribute to a richer, more memorable travel experience. You'll leave Skopelos with stories and souvenirs that are truly distinctive.

How to Support Local Businesses

- Shop Local: Choose local shops and markets for your souvenirs and gifts. Look for items that are handcrafted or unique to Skopelos.

- Dine at Local Restaurants: Opt for dining at family-owned tavernas and restaurants rather than international chains. Enjoy traditional Greek dishes and local specialties.

- Use Local Services: Whether you need a tour guide, rental services, or other activities, choose local providers who contribute to the island's economy.

- Spread the Word: Share your positive experiences and recommendations with others, both online and offline. Word-of-mouth support helps local businesses thrive.

Supporting local businesses in Skopelos is a meaningful way to enhance your travel experience while contributing positively to the island's community and economy. By making informed choices and prioritizing local enterprises, you help preserve Skopelos's unique character, enjoy authentic experiences, and create lasting memories. Your support makes a difference in ensuring that Skopelos remains a vibrant and thriving destination for future visitors.

CONCLUSION

Final Thoughts

As you prepare for your journey to Skopelos, it's important to reflect on the island's unique allure and the experiences that await you. This travel guide aims to equip you with comprehensive information and insights to make your visit both memorable and enriching. Skopelos, with its lush landscapes, crystal-clear waters, and charming villages, offers a distinct blend of natural beauty, cultural heritage, and authentic Greek experiences.

Embracing Skopelos's Unique Charm

Skopelos stands out as a serene and picturesque destination in the Aegean, offering a respite from the more crowded Greek islands. Its landscape is characterized by verdant hills, beautiful beaches, and crystal-clear waters, creating an idyllic setting for relaxation and exploration. The island's historic charm is evident in its traditional architecture, cobblestone streets, and centuries-old monasteries, which provide a window into its rich cultural heritage.

Planning Your Visit

When planning your trip to Skopelos, consider the timing of your visit to make the most of the island's offerings. The best times to visit are during the shoulder seasons of late spring and early autumn, when the weather is pleasant, and the crowds are thinner. This allows you to fully appreciate the island's natural beauty and local culture without the peak-season hustle.

Pack appropriately for the diverse experiences Skopelos offers, from beach days and hiking adventures to exploring historic sites and enjoying local cuisine. Essentials include comfortable walking shoes, sun protection, and a reusable water bottle to stay hydrated during your outdoor activities.

Experiencing the Local Culture
Skopelos is a haven for those seeking authentic Greek experiences. Supporting local businesses is not just a choice; it's a way to immerse yourself in the island's culture. By shopping at local markets, dining at family-owned tavernas, and engaging with local artisans, you contribute to the island's economy and help preserve its unique character.

Respecting local customs and etiquette is crucial for a harmonious interaction with residents. Simple gestures, such as dressing modestly when visiting religious sites and showing politeness in social interactions, go a long way in fostering positive relationships and gaining a deeper appreciation for the island's cultural norms.

Exploring Hidden Gems
While Skopelos has its share of popular attractions, some of its most rewarding experiences lie off the beaten path. Discovering lesser-known beaches, quaint villages, and scenic hiking trails allows you to experience the island's true essence and avoid the more tourist-heavy spots. Embrace the tranquility of secluded coves, the beauty of local monasteries, and the charm of traditional villages to make your visit truly special.

Engaging in Responsible Travel
As with any destination, practicing responsible and eco-friendly travel is essential. Respecting the environment, minimizing waste, and supporting sustainable practices helps preserve Skopelos's natural beauty for future generations. Simple actions, such as disposing of trash properly, avoiding single-use plastics, and choosing eco-friendly accommodations, contribute to a positive impact on the island's ecosystem.

Creating Lasting Memories
Skopelos is more than just a destination; it's an experience that resonates long after you leave. Whether you're savoring the flavors of local

cuisine, exploring ancient ruins, or simply relaxing on a sun-drenched beach, the memories you create here will be cherished. Engage with the local community, immerse yourself in the island's culture, and take the time to appreciate its natural wonders.

Skopelos, remember that the island offers a diverse range of experiences that cater to both relaxation and adventure. From its stunning landscapes and historic sites to its vibrant local culture and cuisine, Skopelos is a destination that promises to captivate and inspire. Approach your visit with an open mind and a spirit of exploration, and you'll find that Skopelos has something truly special to offer.

Thank you for choosing this guide as your companion on your Skopelos adventure. We hope it helps you navigate the island with ease and enjoy all that it has to offer. May your time on Skopelos be filled with discovery, joy, and unforgettable experiences. Safe travels!

Printed in Great Britain
by Amazon